Reading *Faith of our Father* was a
over, behind each of these sermo
text of Scripture including labor
author has a real knack for integr
in order to bring the patriarchal narratives home.

BRYAN D. ESTELLE,
Professor of Old Testament, Westminster Seminary, Escondido California

What a pleasure it is to read Dale Ralph Davis on Abraham.
Once again he takes a Biblical story and presents it in a fresh
and enticing way. He points out details you'd never noticed,
makes connections you'd never thought of, and draws applica-
tions that lead you on in living for God. He writes with clarity,
insight and warmth as well as a lovely humility before God and
his word. Read, enjoy and benefit.

GRAHAM BEYNON,
Pastor, Grace Church Cambridge and
Director of Independent Ministry Training, Oak Hill College.

Faith of our Father is another example of the lively biblical exposition that readers of Dale Ralph Davis have come to know and
love. Each chapter follows the literary contours of the passage
in view, marvels at the grandeur of the God revealed therein,
and brings the consoling and converting powers of the gospel to
bear upon the Christian life. Anyone wanting to study, preach,
or teach Genesis 12-25 will want to have this book ready at hand.

Scott R. Swain,
Professor of Systematic Theology,
Reformed Theological Seminary, Orlando, Florida

Ralph Davis is probably my favorite Old Testament expositor:
he always unfolds the text with freshness, insight, and humor,
leaving the reader with a clear understanding of what God is
up to and the difference that should make in our lives. This
volume on Abraham is a classic in the making!

Iain Duguid,
Professor of Old Testament,
Westminster Theological Seminary, Philadelphia, Pennsylvania

FAITH
OF OUR
FATHER
EXPOSITIONS OF GENESIS 12-25

DALE RALPH DAVIS

CHRISTIAN
FOCUS

CONTENTS

PREFACE

These expositions of Genesis 12–25 were preached as Sunday evening sermons at First Presbyterian Church, Columbia, South Carolina. I have smoothed them out a little but have excluded formal footnoting so as not to interrupt the flow of exposition.

I was perfectly (well, almost) happy in the hills of Tennessee when Derek Thomas, who sometimes can bring turmoil out of peace, contacted me simply to think about helping out with the preaching at Columbia. One item led to another, and now we are living in South Carolina, where I never intended to live, and preaching at First Presbyterian Church, where I never intended to preach. But what a receptive bunch of believers gather on Sunday nights to hear the word! There is always a bit of agony in preaching, but these Sunday evening folks make it worthwhile. So it is only appropriate that I send forth the printed form of these expositions as a tribute to the Sunday evening congregation of First Presbyterian Church, Columbia.

DALE RALPH DAVIS
February 2015

1

God so loved the world that He called Abraham

(Genesis 12:1-9)

He had little choice. The young Frenchman had to leave his homeland. He'd decided he would head for Strasbourg or Basel and find a refuge where he could study and write. But he could not travel straight eastward. It was 1536 and Francis I and Charles V were having their third war and roads were plugged with war materiel. He must detour to the south, through Lyon, angle to the east and approach his destination from the south. He had hoped to reach Lausanne on a certain day but failed— he would have to stay in Geneva. There a fiery William Farel waylaid this Frenchman, John Calvin, and threatened him with God's judgment if he did not remain and assist with the reformation in that place (Thea Van Halsema, *This Was John Calvin*). One doesn't think too much of a war between Francis and Charles, I suppose, until one considers what a huge impact that 'little' circumstance had on Geneva, the Protestant faith, and indeed, the world. In the same way, one might not see huge significance in God's call of a single individual until one realizes that that call will bring blessing to 'all the families of the ground' (v. 3). It was all part of a promise that God gave Abraham. Speaking of that promise, we need to unpack the contents of that promise before we go on.

I call this the 'quad' promise because it consists of four components. First, *people*; Yahweh tells Abram he will make him into a 'great nation' (v. 2) and assures him he will have 'seed' (v. 7). Second, *place*; he tells him he will have a home, the land that Yahweh 'will show you' (v. 1), which turns out to be Canaan (vv. 5b-7). Third, *protection*; he seeks to settle Abram with 'I will bless your blessers, and the one who disdains you I will curse' (v. 3a). Sometimes this 'protection' element is cast in terms of *presence*, as in Genesis 28:15: 'I am with you, and I shall keep you wherever you go.' Finally, this promise contains a *program:* 'and in you all the families of the ground shall be blessed' (v. 3b)—Abram will be the 'funnel' through which/whom blessing comes to the world. God is dead set on blessing his world and he begins that program by calling this man we've just met, and I want you to consider that call.

Before all else, we must understand that this call is **utterly unexplainable** (vv. 1-3). You notice how our chapter begins: 'And Yahweh said to Abram...' Those are the most difficult words to explain. Harder to explain than the mysteries of Melchizedek, harder than Hebrews 6:4-6, far harder than what it might mean to be 'baptized for the dead' in 1 Corinthians 15. Let me explain why I can't explain the words in the first clause of verse 1.

I can't explain them *historically*. Since this is Genesis 12 we know that Genesis 1-11 comes before this chapter. That's a big problem, for there we read of the three-fold crisis of the fall (ch. 3), the flood (chs. 6-8), and the tower (11:1-9)—all of which presents us with a world that is pleased to do without Yahweh's kingship and fellowship, a world that was therefore cursed (ch. 3), destroyed (chs. 6-8), and scattered (11:8-9). So the end should come, the Judge should appear, the hot lava of divine judgment should petrify the world. Why does Yahweh give this world that mocks, defies, and rejects him the promise of blessing (note that root five times in vv. 2-3)? God insists on blessing this world ('all the families of the ground', v. 3b) with Abram as the channel of blessing—he will start all over again with one man as the funnel of redemption. He has in view what Revelation 7:9 depicts: 'a great multitude that no one could number, from every nation, from all tribes and peoples and languages, standing before the throne and before the Lamb.'

But why? It brings to mind something that happened in my family long before I was extant. My oldest brother, Walt, was a wee lad and had some toys, cars and trucks that were in various stages of disrepair. For example, the wheels had been lost, and so when he 'drove' them over the floor in the house the parts that once held the axles and wheels dug into the wood and marred the floor. Naturally, my father didn't like that, but being a good father and seeing no need to try reasoning with a child, he simply picked up those beaten-up toys when Walt was not around and heaved them under the porch. Some days later Pop heard Walt crying and, upon investigating, found that he was trapped under the porch! How he had gotten under there, he could not discern, but Walt was unable to get himself out. But before he would allow my father to extricate him, he handed out to him through the lattice every one of those useless, destructive toys which he had found there. What was it about those worthless things? I can't explain it. He simply wanted them. And who knows why God insists on blessing this violent, rebellious world? Why does he want any truck with it? I can't explain that.

But then I can't explain this call *personally*. We have to watch how we think about Abraham. I have the sneaking suspicion that many Bible readers form an unconscious image of Abraham—they have warm feelings about him, think of him as a gentle sort of fellow, the kind of man they'd want as grandfather for their children. I may be wrong. It's just a hunch. Watchers of old movies in the States might associate him with the likes of Jimmy Stewart, the 'aw shucks', wholesome sort of fellow that folks cannot fail to like, a really 'swell joe.' But, if so, it leads us astray. That's not the Bible's view. Joshua gives us the true view when he repeats Yahweh's words to Israel in Joshua 24:2: 'Your fathers lived on the other side of the River long ago, Terah, the father of Abraham and the father of Nahor, *and they served other gods*' (emphasis mine). That was Abraham. Why did God call Abraham the sinner, Abraham the pagan, Abraham the idolater? It defies logic.

Maybe an analogy will help us to 'get' it. Sergeant R. B. Reed served in the U. S. Army Air Forces during World War II. He was a tail gunner in a Consolidated B-24 Liberator and his crew was making a bombing run over Bolzano, Italy. They were hit by flak that ripped their oxygen lines to shreds. Then came a hit behind the radio cubicle. The waist section of the plane was in flames and that's where Reed's parachute was! So he hurried to get up there and grab his chute. In his hurry he tore his oxygen lines. He could later recall the searing heat and his trouble breathing. He blacked out. Back in the tail section of the bomber.

Not to worry, for he woke up when a rush of cold air hit him. He was speeding earthward in the tail of the B-24 that had become detached from the stricken plane. He was plunging to earth from 22,000 feet without a parachute. Naturally one's mind becomes cluttered with thoughts. One wants to get it over with—and, then again, maybe not. In any case, with a jarring crash the tail rammed through a clump of trees and came to rest on the ground below. Reed opened his eyes and realized he was lying in the snow in one piece. His face was burned and he'd suffered bruises but no bones were broken. A German patrol soon came by and took him prisoner—

the nervous reaction of his ordeal made him weak and very 'capturable' (Brian Kelly, *Best Little Stories from World War II*).

Please understand. I'm very happy for Sgt Reed. I don't wish him ill. At the same time, any reasonable person has to say that that shouldn't happen. When someone falls from over four miles up without a parachute he should become human mush. One is tempted to say that there is something wrong when one does that without even a broken bone. In one sense, it's simply not 'right.'

It's unexplainable—like the call of Abraham (remember Joshua 24:2). And it's no different with you. If you think you know why God has shown his grace to you, then you don't know yourself and you haven't the foggiest idea what grace is. 'But God chose the foolish things of the world...God chose the weak things of the world...God chose the insignificant things of the world and the despised things, the things that are nothing...' (1 Cor. 1:27ff.). Or one can sing with the hymn that begins, 'I know not why God's wondrous grace, to me he hath made known.'

This call is utterly unexplainable. You start here or you won't get anywhere. You can't explain why there's a call at all—why the gracious God should show grace to you at all.

But, secondly, you must notice that this call is **quietly successful** (vv. 4-5, 7b-9). How was it successful? Well, in the simplicity of Abram's obedience, as verses 4-5 show. These verses tell a good bit: who went on the journey, how old Abram was at the time, the destination. Yet the keynote comes in 4a, in that simple low-key report: 'So Abram went as Yahweh had spoken to him.' Notice, by the way, how much is left out, how very 'economical' the Bible is in this report. The journey was a major undertaking, but there is not a word about the precise route or the various weather conditions encountered, nothing about whether they had to fend off brigands or whether they traveled with a larger caravan or whether they ate at Dairy

Queens or Chick-fil-As. None of that. Abram went as Yahweh had spoken to him—in spite of family ties (v. 1), and his own age perhaps (v. 4), and perhaps uncertainty about his destination, at least at first (cf. Heb. 11:8). 'As Yahweh had spoken to him.' Nothing much matters but obeying his word.

The late Jean Cadier, a French Reformed scholar, tells how this matter came home to one of his students. After a lecture in theological college, one of Prof. Cadier's students came up and told him that he had been converted by reading Calvin's *Institutes*. Of course Cadier was curious—what 'message' was it exactly that had gotten through to this fellow? The student responded by saying that 'I learnt from reading Calvin that all the fears about health and the uncertain future that had hitherto dominated my life were without much importance, and that the only thing that mattered was obedience to the will of God and a care for his glory.' The simplicity of his obedience. 'So Abram went as Yahweh had spoken to him.'

But then we also see the success of this call in the shame-lessness of his worship (vv. 7b-9). Abram arrived at Shechem in the center of Canaan. Verse 6 mentions the oak of Moreh; that could be translated 'the oak [or, terebinth] of the teacher'; it may have been a pagan sacred spot, perhaps where devotees claimed to receive 'revelation' at the 'teacher tree.' But in spite of the pagan trappings, Abram builds 'an altar to Yahweh who had appeared to him' (v. 7b). He doesn't mesh with the local liturgy, doesn't blend with the going religious gig. He worships Yahweh only and openly.

It happens again when he camps further south between Bethel and Ai: 'he built there an altar to Yahweh and called on the name of Yahweh' (v. 8b). Here are twin elements of worship: atonement (altar) and testimony ('called'). A few commentators make a big deal out of the fact that it says Abram built an altar but it doesn't say he offered sacrifice. I don't get why they seem to hope Abram didn't sacrifice, but really, what is an altar for? If he built an altar why wouldn't he sacrifice? It's like a home-maker writing her sister and telling her that she and her husband were getting the evening meal ready; her husband was grilling filet mignon outside and she herself was making a salad of greens with their favorite dressing, cooking some asparagus, and baking some blond brownies to go with the home-made ice cream they had made earlier in the day. What if her sister read that note and responded, 'Well, quite a meal, but *it doesn't say that they ate it!*' But sometimes assumptions are as clear as assertions.

So Abram sacrifices; he comes to God by means of atonement, by the offering of another in his place. The other part of his worship is a bit unclear. Some render the text as 'calling on the name of Yahweh,' referring to some form of public prayer and worship, while others hold that, especially in these first books of the Bible, the verb should not be translated 'calling' but 'proclaiming'—Abram may have been proclaiming truth about Yahweh, about his character and graciousness. However it is taken, the text still speaks of testimony given in open and public worship. Openly and unabashed in Canaanite culture, Abram seeks or testifies of Yahweh. He pitched his tent and built an altar. Someone has said that tent and altar rather characterize Abram's life; tent speaks of his life as a pilgrim, often on the move, while altar speaks of him as a worshiper; tent indicates he sits light on circumstances, altar that he holds fast to the essential.

What is the import of all this? My normal tendency would be to ignore this part of the narrative, simply because I follow an unwritten rule that it's better to keep one's focus on God and what he's doing in a narrative than on man and his responses. Yet this record of Abram's response is here for a reason. It tells us that God's call has takers! Like Abram. Surely God wants a people who respond to his call. One suspects that this record is here because Abram's response is the sort of response God is seeking from us as well. It may have been heart-wrenching (cf. v. 1), but the report of Abram's response is simply so ordinary, so matter-of-fact—not as though there is much dramatic or spectacular about it at all. That's often the way Christ's call upon us plays out—nothing necessarily earth-shaking or fantastic. Christ probably won't call you to go to seminary, it's almost a sure thing that he won't call you to go as a missionary to Nepal; he may not be too concerned whether you become an officer in your local church or whether you start up a new para-church ministry. No, all that matters is that his word directs us (that's verse 4a) and that his worship preoccupies us (that's verse 8b).

Finally, this call is **seemingly impossible** (vv. 6-7). God's plan to bless the world with a Savior through Abram looks like it will never get off the ground. It sounds good in its promise form in verse 2 ('I will make you into a great nation'), but when Yahweh enlarges and re-affirms it in verse 7 ('To your seed I will give this land') it flies in the teeth of reality. That little squib about the Canaanites being in the land in verse 6 was no useless bit of filler; it tells you that the land is already in the possession of others, so how will it get to belong to Abram's seed? So much for the place-promise. But it doesn't look any better for the people-promise. 'To your seed,' Yahweh says, but we already know that Abram doesn't have any seed and is not likely to get any since Sarai is barren (11:30). So verse 7a packs it all into one impossible sentence, for Abram has no seed and the land belongs to others. Looks like this call was all for nothing. But as I think Derek Kidner reminds us, God's way is to preface his great works with extreme difficulties. Sometimes it simply *has* to be that way.

It all reminds me of a story Martyn Lloyd-Jones told about an incident in his childhood (see Iain Murray's first volume of L-J's biography, 1:10). Martyn's father was keen to sell a separator to a couple of farmers. Martyn was perhaps ten years old and he was with his father as they took the pony and trap and went about six miles out of their village to this farm. The farmers there were two brothers, both unmarried, and the older one was the 'master.' He was quite conservative and not at all open to purchasing any separator. The younger brother was eager to purchase it, but he was, alas, the younger brother. No sooner had Lloyd-Jones and son turned into the lane that led to the farmhouse than the younger brother appeared and greeted them. He told Mr Lloyd-Jones, 'There's only one way for you to sell that separator and that is if I speak strongly against it. I was anxious for you not to misunderstand me when I start to object.' With that he disappears. So they head on down the lane, meet up with the older brother and begin talking business. After about ten minutes when any possibility of a deal is at best bleak, the younger brother comes round with a rather grim look on his face. The older brother asked him what he thought of the separator, and he immediately began to speak vehemently against it. Needless to say, Martyn said, we sold the separator! The difficulty and the hopelessness were a necessary part of the procedure.

That is often the built-in component with God's promises as well. God not only operates this way with Abram but with many of his servants as well. We must be careful here: he does not *always* work this way, but he has a *tendency* to do so. This is *a pattern God repeats with his people* throughout their history and experience, not just corporately but individually. Take merely one example. Look at 2 Corinthians 1:8-10a, where Paul remembers being reduced to helplessness: *For we do not want you to be unaware, brothers, of the affliction we experienced in Asia. For we were so utterly burdened beyond our strength that we despaired of life itself. Indeed, we felt that we had received the sentence of death. But that was to make us rely not on ourselves but on God who raises the dead. He delivered us from such a deadly peril, and he will deliver us* (ESV).

Now I know I am speaking very generally here. But God tends to do this. He tends to put his people in impossible situations, so boxed in by unchangeable circumstances that appear 'un-tweakable', reduced to such helplessness that there's no strength or energy to find a way out—all to teach us that if we survive, if we endure, if we go on standing in the mess, it is only by his power that we do so and not by our own cleverness, for we are quite overwhelmed. God seems to stamp 'seemingly impossible' on far more than Abram's original call.

So...God so loved the world that he called Abraham. And he keeps adding to Abraham's seed, gathering more and more of Abraham's children—and he is *still* gathering people to share Abraham's faith. The call he gave Abraham has not really changed; what Yahweh demanded of Abraham in verse 1 is really quite like what Jesus demands of us in, say, Matthew 10:37-38: *The one who loves father or mother more than me is not worthy of me; and the one who loves son or daughter more than me is not worthy of me; and whoever does not take his cross and follow after me is not worthy of me.* Sounds different from Genesis 12:1, but it's really the same. Jesus is simply demanding the place of supreme affection in your life. That's all. So what is it that's keeping you from coming to the One who calls you?

2

GOD KEEPS HOLD OF LOSERS
(Genesis 12:10–13:4)

In John Bunyan's *Pilgrim's Progress* Christian and Hopeful turn aside into Bypath Meadow, where they are found and captured by Giant Despair, who takes them to Doubting Castle. He throws them into the dungeon there without any food or water or light. He urges the pilgrims to do away with themselves because their fate is sealed. Hopeful argues Christian out of taking that option. But all is bleak. Once the giant takes them to the courtyard and shows them the remains of previous specimens he had torn apart; he tells them that in ten days he will do the same to them. On Saturday night, about midnight, the two pilgrims begin to pray and pray on almost till dawn. And suddenly Christian exclaims, 'What a fool am I, thus to lie in a stinking dungeon, when I may as well walk at liberty! I have a key in my bosom called Promise; that will, I am persuaded, open any lock in Doubting Castle.' It worked on the dungeon door; it worked on the outward door to the castle-yard; and, though the lock worked hard, even the iron gate to the whole complex opened. And off they went, back to the King's Highway.

Now Abram had a key called Promise, but he didn't use it. No sooner, it seems, does Abram receive Yahweh's promises

(12:1-9) than he fails to trust the Promiser (12:10-20). I say it seems that way; it's all packed into one chapter, but we don't know the exact time frame. It may be that the episodes in 12:10-20 happened after the passage of some time. It's simply that when the whole story is scrunched into one chapter it gives the appearance that Abraham's un-faith followed fairly quickly upon his faith. In any case, here in Genesis 12:10–13:4 faith faces the fear of man. I have no slick approach to this passage; I simply want to highlight the teaching of this passage to God's people, who, like Abraham, are promise recipients.

First, our passage implies that **God laces our lives with his strange pattern**: 'Now there was a famine in the land; so Abram went down to Egypt to sojourn there, for the famine was severe in the land' (v. 10 ESV). As someone has said, 'land' is mentioned twice in this short verse. Back in verse 7 the land was promised to Abram's seed, and now Abram must leave the land. The land is a promise, and yet the land is a problem. Famine. Yahweh promised that land and now the promise seems threatened. Sometimes it appears that way— God makes promises and yet those promises appear so fragile. God may assure you of something (v. 7), and then something comes along that places question marks after that assurance.

In the *Peanuts* cartoons one finds Linus gun-shy of this 'pattern.' Lucy is reading to Linus from a book: 'And so the King was granted his wish—everything he touched would turn to gold! Now, the next day....' Linus jumps to his feet and exclaims, 'Stop! You don't have to read any further! I know just what's going to happen.' Off he goes, muttering, 'These things always have a way of backfiring!' It looks that way with the land: Abram is promised the land for his seed, but then he can't even stay in the land.

But if this pattern is strange, it's also a bit common. Remember Jesus at his baptism; remember that marvelous assurance he received from the Father: 'You are my Son, the One I love; I am delighted with you!' (Mark 1:11). No sooner does Mark record that than he uses his favorite adverb, 'immediately'—'Immediately the Spirit drives him out into the wilderness, and he was in the wilderness forty days, being tempted by Satan' (vv. 12-13). How can we hope to fathom the comfort that must've washed over Jesus when he heard his Father's words in verse 11—and then 'immediately' desolation and temptation. Great assurance but then severe test. Or think of Paul in 2 Corinthians 12. Such an ecstatic experience he had—caught up to the third heaven, into Paradise, hearing matters that could not be told (vv. 1-4). Who knows what that was like? But then, to keep him from becoming conceited or too elated over receiving these revelations, Paul was given a 'thorn in the flesh,' apparently some debilitating physical condition, to torment him (v. 7). That strange pattern.

New Year's Day 1773. William Cowper was walking over the fields around Olney when he sensed that another period of darkness and depression was going to come over him. He rushed home and immediately wrote down an expression of his faith in a hymn. You are familiar with much of it.

> *God moves in a mysterious way,*
> *His wonders to perform;*
> *He plants his footsteps in the sea*
> *And rides upon the storm.*
>
> *Ye fearful saints, fresh courage take;*
> *The clouds ye so much dread*
> *Are big with mercy and shall break*
> *In blessings on your head.*
>
> *Judge not the Lord by feeble sense,*
> *But trust him for his grace;*
> *Behind a frowning providence*
> *He hides a smiling face.*

But Cowper saw no smiling face the next day. His friend John Newton went to visit him and found him delirious and full of terror. In these days Cowper didn't seem to notice what was going on around him. He still went for walks with Newton but the latter had to direct him as if Cowper were a mannequin (cf. George Ella, *William Cowper: Poet of Paradise*). But there is that strange pattern again: fine assurance then deep darkness.

This is one reason I love the word of God—it is so unbendingly honest. It hides nothing from me. So take it from Genesis 12: there will be times when the promises of God look doubtful, times when they may seem to have more question marks after them than exclamation points.

Secondly, verses 11-16 teach that **God's promise must be rubbed into our fearful circumstances**. These verses begin by telling us of the problem (v. 11), the peril (v. 12), and the policy (v. 13). The problem is that Abraham has married a beautiful woman. That's the dilemma. Abram tells Sarai, 'Look, I know that you are a beautiful woman.' The text tempts us to go on a tangent. You notice that Abram never talks until verse 11. Oh, I'm sure he talked, but these are the very first words he is recorded to have said in Scripture—and his first words spoken complimented his wife on how beautiful she was! More men should take their cue from Abram and tell their wives how beautiful they are. Assuming they can truthfully say it! But unless a man was completely out to lunch, as we say, he must have been highly attracted by the one who became his wife. And it might help one's marriage if he periodically took a page from Abram's playbook and told his wife how attractive she is.

A beautiful woman can be a problem. Abram thought so; he was sure that when the Egyptians gave Sarai the eye, they would want to liquidate him as her husband in order to have her (v. 12). But this danger could be overcome if Sarai would claim she was Abram's sister (v. 13). Actually, that was a partial truth, for they both had the same father (20:12), but it was meant as an intentional deception. It's a bit akin to underage lads who wanted to fight in our War between the States. The minimal age for enlistment was eighteen, but some fellows would take slips of paper and write '18' on them and slip them into their shoes. When asked how old they were, they could 'truthfully' answer, 'I'm over 18.'

For all the deception one could say there is a bit of faith in this. If the promise was to come true (of the seed and land), Abram must live. He's seeking to ensure that. But what of Sarai? Is he throwing her to the dogs? He seems certainly to be putting her at risk, but he may have had a plan. Now here we hark back to an old explanation. It may or may not be right. Whenever we do this we go 'behind' the text and pull stuff in that's not explicitly in the text, so we have to say that we don't really know; the text doesn't explicitly say. But the explanation is that Abram may have calculated that if anyone had designs on Sarai, they would have to negotiate with her 'brother,' and in that process Abram would be able to delay and frustrate and draw out the process and be in 'control' somewhat. That may well have been, but he may not have counted on Pharaoh wanting Sarai; Pharaoh's lackeys tell him what a dish Sarai is and she is swept off to his harem. Kings don't have to negotiate with brothers or with anyone; they take what they want. It is likely that Abram didn't consider a scenario with Pharaoh in it.

But give Abram credit for some savvy. Basically what Abram predicted in verses 11-12 happened in verse 14-16. He was no dummy; he was smart. We could say, however, that though he was accurate, he was not faithful; he was basically right and yet grossly wrong.

The major problem here is not Abram's deception but his unbelief. He failed to believe the promise of verse 3a and rub it into his circumstances. That was the 'protection clause' of the promise ('I will bless your blessers, and the one who disdains you I will curse'). How should he have approached the matter?

Well, he should have said to Sarai, 'My dear, I know you're a real doll and that could be a real problem in Egypt; but we have a promise from Yahweh, and, even though this sojourn in Egypt carries some risks, we must simply lean on Yahweh's promise and commit our safety to him.' The promise of God should have cast out the fear of man. But Abram did not take that tack; it's as if he says, 'No, God's promise is not enough; this calls for my ingenuity.' That is not so unusual. Most of us have 'been there.' We have the promises of God but we don't rub them into our circumstances. It's not lack of knowledge; we know the promises and assurances; we simply don't apply what we know in the situation we're in. I always think of an embarrassing occasion of this kind of thing.

My wife and I were serving in our first pastorate in a small town in northeastern Kansas. Our first baby was still, I believe, less than a year old when we had an ice storm and the electricity was knocked out. We had no other means of heat in the manse except the furnace, and, though it was not an electric furnace, it did have an electric switch, so with the power off it did not work. We began to wonder what we would do if the power was off indefinitely. How would we keep our baby warm and so on. Now one of the elders in the church owned a hardware store up on the town square, and suddenly I had an idea. I told my wife, 'If this power outage goes on, I'll just go up to Broky's Hardware and buy one of those space heaters that you plug in and we can put it in the family room....' It was an interesting and illogical idea. I *knew* that the power was out—why was I thinking of getting an electrical space heater of all things? I simply didn't rub my knowledge into the circumstances. That was Abram's problem as well.

I know I am only dealing generally here. That's really all I can do just now. But we ourselves have a sort of Abraham-type assurance from Jesus—you can check it out in Matthew 10:28 (and context): 'And do not fear those who kill the body but cannot kill the soul. Rather fear him who can destroy both soul and body in hell'(ESV). And we know, don't we, how torturous it can prove to rub that assurance into the pores of our souls in the middle of those times when we are fearing other people. It may not be anything near 'killing the body'; it may be simply someone who can fire us from our job and apparent livelihood. And we need to rub Jesus' word into our circumstances.

Thirdly, verse 17 tells us that **only God's power can guarantee God's plan**. 'Then Yahweh struck Pharaoh with great plagues, along with his household, because of Sarai, Abram's wife.' We have all sorts of questions, and there are all sorts of details that we simply don't have. What sort of plagues? How did Pharaoh find out the reason? Did he have relations with Sarai? Lots we don't know. But we know that Yahweh was true to his word in verse 3a, which, rather bluntly put, means, 'You mess with Abraham, you answer to me.'

It was what we might call muscular intervention. Sometimes you need something like that. You would find this sort of thing at least in the older days of American baseball. In 1969 the Chicago Cubs came to New York to play a series with the Mets before over 43,000 fans. A pitcher by the name of Hands was throwing for the Cubs. When Hands faced the first Mets' batter he threw at his head. The batter barely got out of the way. So when the Cubs came to bat next, the Mets' pitcher, Koosman, threw a fastball at the batter, Ron Santo, and drilled him in the arm. He threw it hard, and they thought perhaps Santo's arm was broken. Koosman went on to strike out the next three shaky batters. Later, Koosman said something like this: 'Our manager, Gil Hodges, once told us pitchers that we needed to "protect" our players. Sometimes you have to send a message to the other team.' And Koosman sent that message; it was as if he was saying, 'You keep throwing at my teammates, and your players will go home with a lot of sore and broken body parts.' A bit intimidating—like Yahweh's plague on Pharaoh and Co.

Verse 17 hits us out of the blue, for Yahweh has been unmentioned and silent throughout the whole episode. It seems as if everything rests on Abram and his schemes. So we are surprised at verse 17—God intervenes directly in such a surprising and unexpected way.

Seeing Yahweh's intervention should produce two attitudes in us. The first is *humility*. At this point we ask, How can Abram be preserved in a hostile world so that he will have a seed that will multiply and be the channel by which God's blessing comes on the whole earth? Well, not by Abram's smarts. This was a fainting fit of faith. Such failure is not surprising perhaps, because God has been making new beginnings all through Genesis so far: in Adam and Seth in Genesis 5, in Noah in Genesis 9, and then with Abram here in chapter 12. But they all, as we sometimes say, go to pot. And Yahweh's Abraham-plan would have gone down the sewer too except that Yahweh determined by his power that he would not allow it to fail in spite of the failures of his servant. There's an 'overflow' here for believers in the church who claim to share Abram's faith: we must realize that we not only share his faith but often his foibles and his fainting fits and his folly and his fears—all of which tells us that when the wash is all in, God's plan and God's kingdom will come because God will see to it and not because we are such outstanding members of Jesus' all-star team.

Then too Yahweh's intervention should produce *hope* in us. Is not the likes of verse 17 the hope of God's people? No, it doesn't mean we have no responsibility, but isn't it good news to know that God's world-blessing plan doesn't rest on any paltry, twisted faithfulness of mine? Why will the church, why will Abraham's seed keep on going? Because God will see to it. Or, as the third stanza of Samuel Stone's splendid hymn ('The Church's One Foundation') tells us: 'The church will never perish—her dear Lord to defend—to guide, sustain, and cherish, is with her to the end....' Only God's power can guarantee God's plan.

Finally, our passage shows us that **God's grace keeps his servants from despair** (12:18-20 and 13:1-4). The interesting feature about Abram's Egypt fiasco and failure is that it's not depressing. Or at least it doesn't strike me that way. Yahweh doesn't come out with an exasperated sigh and tell Abram he's blown his opportunity, and that he, Yahweh, will have to look for another servant to carry his flag in the world. And he didn't abandon Abram or tell him he could fry in his own juice. Of course, there is the shame of verses 18-20—Abram is forcibly deported and he doesn't come out with a fantastic 'testimony.' But notice 13:1-4, especially the careful geography of verses 3-4, and the emphasis on 'at the beginning' and 'at the first.' *And he went by stopping places from the south country all the way to Bethel, to the place where his tent had been at the beginning, between Bethel and Ai, to the place of the altar he had made at the first, and there Abram called on the name of Yahweh.* Back to Bethel. Back to the altar. Such places are important.

George Whitefield always remembered where his new birth occurred. He said: 'I know the place! It may be superstitious, perhaps, but whenever I go to Oxford I cannot help running to that place where Jesus Christ first revealed himself to me and gave me the new birth' (Arnold Dallimore, *George Whitefield*, 1:77). And the Puritan Walter Pringle speaks of having committed his new born son to God 'at the plum tree on the north side of the garden door' (L. Ryken, *Worldly Saints*, 209). Places are important and ought to be remembered. And this altar at Bethel is important. It's as if Abram is purposely going back to start all over again, as if his geography is an expression of his repentance. Remember the significance of the altar— it is the place where atonement is made by the offering of a substitute. Abram goes back and starts all over again there.

There were some revivals in East Anglia in England in the 1920s. They aren't often spoken of but were really quite significant. Douglas Brown was one of the primary preachers and leaders in those renewing times. He once very helpfully described what revival was; he said revival 'is not going down the street with a big drum, it is going back to Calvary with a big sob' (I. Murray, *Archibald G. Brown: Spurgeon's Successor*, 332).

That's what you are to do. Oh, you say, but my fainting fit brought such shame on Christ's name; or, you say, I have so miserably failed and in the process my waywardness and wickedness has devastated the lives of people I loved; or, you say, Surely Christ wants no truck with someone who has been so stupid and stubborn. Well, go back to the cross of Jesus and find out—because that's where God keeps hold of losers.

3

RESIDENT OR PILGRIM?

Genesis 13:5-18

Sometimes when we give our order at a 'fast food' restaurant, the clerk will ask, 'What's the name for the order?' Note: she does not ask what is *my* name, but 'What is the name for the order?' So, of course, it can be any name—just so she can identify the order. So I will say 'Tony' or 'George' or whatever name I conjure up. Of course, in that case it's important to remember who you are. If they call out 'Sam' or 'Louie' and you have forgotten you 'are' one of them, your food could get cold.

Sometimes, however, other people may tell you who you are. I remember one of the first faculty meetings I attended when I first began to teach at a Christian college in the deep south of the United States. I'm originally a northerner, and, if I have an accent, it is certainly not a southern one. One of the women on the faculty said to me, I think in jest, 'You talk funny.' Whether in jest or more sinister it basically meant, 'You don't belong, you're different.'

And, in one sense, that's what the Bible says about God's people—we don't belong and we shouldn't get too settled down into the system of things. It says to us, Remember who you are. In fact, the Bible calls us 'pilgrims' (at least in the NKJV):

'Beloved, I beg you as sojourners and pilgrims, abstain from fleshly lusts which war against the soul' (1 Peter 2:11); or, 'These all [including Abraham and Co.] died in faith, not having received the promises, but having seen them afar off were assured of them, embraced them, and confessed that they were strangers and pilgrims on the earth' (Heb. 11:13 NKJV). Genesis 13 is concerned about this; its main point is that *covenant people must be careful to remain pilgrims*, and they do so partly by distrusting appearances and welcoming promises.

We need to catch up on our story line. Abram and Lot are back in Canaan from Egypt and they have a positive problem (vv. 5-6). They are both very well off and have much livestock (vv. 2, 5). But that makes it difficult to stay in close proximity, for there's usually a limited amount of grazing land and water sources in a localized area. Not surprisingly, quarrels broke out between their hired men (v. 7)—and these relatives couldn't afford the luxury of disputes if they wanted to put up a united front in face of the Canaanites and Perizzites around them (v. 7b). So Abram made his gracious proposal that they separate—Lot could choose his spot first and Abram would go elsewhere (vv. 8-9).

So...*covenant people must be careful to remain pilgrims*. But how does one recognize a pilgrim? Do they really talk funny or act weirdly or wear 1970s leisure suits or don't use computers or sport suspenders that don't match? We can try to answer that negatively (in terms of Lot) and positively (in terms of Abram).

First, notice that in Lot's response we seem to have **the antithesis of a pilgrim** (vv. 10-13). Indeed, there seems to be a certain irony in verse 10, when it says that 'Lot lifted up his eyes and saw....' No, that's the problem. He really didn't see. He saw the advantages (v. 10a) but not the dangers (v. 13), he saw the perks but not the perils. A few years ago, one of the political campaigns in the United States ran on the slogan, 'It's the economy, stupid.'

And Lot seems to have had his eye primarily on the economy; he seems to have been really drawn to the place ('he pitched his tent as far as Sodom,' v. 12b). We readers cringe because we see these hints of trouble, these shadows of disaster in verses 10b and 13. They make us worry over Lot's decision.

You may not have noticed but in the margin of your Bible there's a little 'fast forward' button. No, actually there's not, but if there were, and if you punched it, it would take you to Genesis 19. I recall a sermon I preached when I was twenty years old on Genesis 19, called 'Lot's Losses.' I wouldn't preach it again now. But there are losses for Lot in Genesis 19; for example, he loses his moral backbone (19:8) and he loses his family for God. And most of that arises from what Lot didn't see in chapter 13.

One can't blame Lot for what he did see. He saw security from famine; he saw the plain of the Jordan and 'how well-irrigated it all was' (v. 10) and that likely meant no more trips to Egypt like in 12:10-20. He saw abundant provision for his livestock. Easy for city folks not to appreciate that. A number of years ago cattle feed lots began to multiply around my wife's hometown in western Kansas. They were perhaps five or six or eight miles from town. But the wind always blows in Kansas and wafts smells on its wings. So if one went out one's front door in town, one met the smell of a feed lot! I remember speaking with a local about that fact once, and he gave me a new perspective: 'It's the smell of money!'

And that may have been what Lot saw and smelled as he viewed the turf on the plain of the Jordan. Perhaps he saw some extra comforts for his family. But he didn't seem to see or sense the hidden dangers that verses 10b and 13 hint of. And what we don't see can be lethal.

That was almost the case in August 1944 in Paris. The allies had swept in, the Germans were driven out. Well, almost. Lieutenant Commander Harry Leithold was holding out, after some fighting, in the corridors of Gabriel's palace. He knew the place intimately and had squirreled himself away in a small room on the corner of the third floor to hide out until night, when he hoped he might escape. Leithold heard a crowd roaring outside. He looked out and saw an open black car coming into the square; he reached down and pulled up his MP submachine gun and cautiously rested it on the window ledge. He was thinking about what foolish chances Frenchmen take, as he saw a French general, hardly 200 yards away, in the back seat of that open car. Leithold fixed the man in his sight and readied to fire. What a momentous way to end his part in the war—knocking off a French general! Then something happened—the crowd broke restraints and ran out to swarm round the car. Leithold realized that if he fired, that crowd would hunt him down and beat him to death. Regretfully he pulled back his submachine gun. At least at the time Charles de Gaulle had no idea that he had come within a whisper of having his brains blown out. What he didn't see was dangerous.

What ought this piece of the story drive home to us? Perhaps that we ought to have a holy distrust of our own wisdom, of our ability to assess our circumstances from our own flat-footed position, of assuming that we 'can handle this.' I'm not psychologizing Lot—who knows how he felt! I'm not assuming that he was overtly arrogant. But there can be a very subtle way we can have about us of looking at circumstances and assuming that we pretty much size them up rightly. That seemed to be going on here.

I can vividly remember once in my childhood when I had a distinct inner feeling of being in control, of being able to handle a situation. I was across the street in our western Pennsylvania town, playing at Eddie Phipps' house. Eddie had to go in to eat supper and so I was left outside in his back yard, waiting for him. I had my baseball bat and a ball and was standing maybe sixty feet from the back of the Phipps' house, at the end of a sidewalk that ran up to their basement door. Ah, yes, the basement door. It had a pane of glass in the top part of it, maybe 18 inches long by 14 wide. The thought went through my head that if I hit my ball toward the house, there was *no way* I could knock out the glass in that basement door. Sometimes one has an arrogance of certainty, and I had it. There was clearly no chance of my being so accurate with a batted ball. But one can't merely hypothesize about these things; one must prove them. So I flipped up my ball, took my left-handed swing, and showed I was right. I smashed the kitchen window where they were eating supper instead! And yet I had been so sure of myself.

Of course, Proverbs 3:5 tells us not to be; we are to trust in the Lord with all our heart and not lean on our own understanding. It doesn't say we shouldn't use our understanding but that we shouldn't lean on it. Sometimes we lean on our understanding and use the Lord. Lot's assessment of things here seemed to be superficial. And so the story pushes us to plead with God for the discernment we need, not to be content with obvious appearances or merely economic factors. We should ask questions like: Will this 'opportunity' calcify my marriage? Will it estrange me or distance me from my family? Will it disrupt worship—personally, domestically, or publicly? Will it de-sensitize me to sin and evil? O Lord, when I lift up my eyes, make me able truly to see.

We now turn, more positively, to **the anatomy of a pilgrim**, as set out in verses 8-9 and 14-18. This piece of the text indicates one can tell a pilgrim by what he has or by what he enjoys.

First, a pilgrim enjoys *the freedom of the providence of God* (vv. 8-9). Abram was magnanimous with Lot; he didn't press his seniority; he gave him, as we say, first crack. This suggests Abram's faith in God's promise. Yahweh had promised the land to Abram's seed (12:7) and Abram seemingly rested in that: no matter what choice Lot made, God would see to the 'promise part.' No need then to try to manipulate things. This episode brings to mind 2 Samuel 15:25-26, when David was fleeing Jerusalem because Absalom was seizing the throne. As David's loyalists were leaving the city, Abiathar and Zadok, the high priests, show up, with some of the Levites. They have the ark of the covenant with them. Absalom may get the city and the throne, in other words, but he won't have the priesthood or the sign of Yahweh's presence. And David calls it all off: 'Take the ark of God back to the city; if I find grace in Yahweh's eyes, he shall bring me back and allow me to see both it and his residence; but if he says, "I do not delight in you"—here I am—let him do to me as seems good to him.'

David so much as says, No, we're not going down that road; we'll walk by faith not by superstition; having God's furniture does not mean I would have God's favor. David's words are not despairing but freeing. Because he places himself within God's providence and under God's grace he doesn't have to try to manipulate him. Pilgrims are folks who say, 'My times are in your hands' (Ps. 31:15) and really believe it.

Second, a pilgrim has *the word of the promise of God* (vv. 14-16). Lot 'lifted up his eyes' in verse 10, and now Yahweh tells Abram to 'lift up your eyes' (v. 14) and look in all directions, 'for,' he says, 'all the land which you are seeing, to you I will give it and to your seed for all time' (v. 15). Abram receives an intensification, or perhaps better, an amplification or expansion of the promise. Something is added to the place-promise: '*to you* and to your seed.' Yahweh had already promised the land to Abram's seed (12:7), but here it is also promised to Abram himself. (We'll look at this further in the exposition of chapter 17). Then there is an 'extra' in the people-promise: Yahweh had already promised to make Abram a 'great nation' (12:2), but here he vows he will make his seed like 'the dust of the earth' (v. 16). Yahweh amplifies the promise. Of course, one could say that the big characteristic of this promise is its 'not yet' character—that's what Hebrews 11:13 underscores. Abraham and others died 'not having received the promises,' meaning they had not received *what* was promised; they received the promises but not what was promised; they held on to the promises, even though they did not see their fulfillment.

You might say, Well, I'm glad we Christian believers are not in that situation. Oh, but we are! True, we live on this side of the empty cross and the empty tomb and the occupied throne from which Jesus reigns at the Father's right hand. But we're in the same Abraham-position. Well, think of what Jesus has told us: 'In my Father's house are many abiding places; if it were not so, I would have told you, because I go to prepare a place for you; and if I go and prepare a place for you, I will come again and take you to be with myself, that where I am, there you may be also' (John 14:2-3). With all our privileges we have not yet received what was promised in that promise. We are standing in Not-yet-land, we are in Abraham's sandals. What keeps one holding on then? The character of the Promiser! Remember Jesus' words: 'If it were not so, I would have told you.'

In 1948 Governor Strom Thurmond of South Carolina broke with the Democratic Party and was nominated for President by the 'Dixiecrats,' whose platform supported racial segregation. Thurmond was displeased with President Harry Truman's promises to support civil rights. Someone asked Thurmond why he would break with the party over this, since Franklin Roosevelt had made the same sort of civil rights assurances as had Truman. Thurmond retorted, 'But Truman really means it' (David McCullough, *Truman*). Makes all the difference, doesn't it? That's what Jesus is saying here with his 'If it were not so, I would have told you' (NIV). Jesus really means it. And that's why pilgrim people go on holding on to the word of the promise of God.

Third, a pilgrim is one who enjoys *the foretaste of the goodness of God*: 'Rise, walk around through the land, down its length and across its breadth, for to you I will give it' (v. 17). One could say Yahweh was giving Abram the 'royal treatment,' for this was the sort of thing kings sometimes did. In Hittite and Egyptian sources the king might have to do a ceremonial walk around a field or a tour of his realm to symbolize the renewal of his sovereignty over the land. Abram's tour was a claiming of his 'dominion,' enjoying a foretaste of what he was to receive. My wife has told me that when she purchases something from the deli section in one of our grocery stores, whoever is serving her always gives her a sample of what she orders. I like Colby cheese, especially for grilled cheese sandwiches—it always melts so 'goo-ily'. So when she asks for a half pound of Colby, the person at the counter gives her a small sample to try. It's not much, it's only a taste, but it's a bit of the same stuff you'll have later. And the Lord is like that with his people—he tends to give them foretastes of what he will do for them, as he did in the land tour in verse 17. Christians may think of their celebration of the Lord's supper. No, it's not Matthew 8:11 yet ('Many will come from the east and west and recline at table with Abraham, Isaac, and Jacob in the kingdom of heaven' ESV), nor is it yet the marriage supper of the Lamb (Rev. 19), but it's a foretaste of what is to come; it is one of the Lord's gracious appetizers. And pilgrims always prize them.

Fourthly, if Abram is any guide, pilgrims enjoy *the privilege of the worship of God*: 'Then Abram moved tent and came and dwelt among the oaks of Mamre which are in Hebron; and he built there an altar to Yahweh' (v. 18). As we've seen in chapters 12 and 13, this is a pattern. Abram always seems to build an altar; he worships on the basis of atoning sacrifice, openly and unashamed. I don't think we should miss this: the man with the promises consistently worships.

I hope we sense the privilege in our public worship. In our current congregational setting, we use a number of time-honored elements in worship, and sometimes we can fail to see the privilege and delight we should find in them. Most Sundays the Doxology is part of worship. That ought to thrill us. In part of that we call on 'all creatures here below' to praise the triune God. Of course that is in line with God's decree that every knee will bow to him and every tongue will acknowledge him (Isa. 45:23); so we call on folks who will have to acknowledge him one way or another to do so voluntarily and join us in praise. And then we talk to the angels! 'Praise him above, ye heavenly hosts!' Nothing abnormal about that; David talked to the angels in this vein in Psalm 103:20. Why shouldn't their praise dwarf and drown ours? What a privilege to stir them up!

Some of us use the Apostles' Creed in worship. When you say the creed you are engaging in an act of defiance, for the Christ you confess is the Christ rejected by the world, by Pontius Pilate and all his lackeys, whether they are non-committal or viciously hostile. But here you have the privilege of saying your 'No' to world opinion; you stick out your jaw and say, 'This crucified, risen, ascended, and coming Christ is mine, and I acknowledge him, no matter what you say.'

But the creed is defiant is another way. Think where people come from when they prepare to say the creed. Where have they been the week before? Some of them have been in grief; they have lost a spouse or loved one; or some have had life tumble in on them in disappointments and troubles. And then they say the creed. What are they saying except that 'I *still* believe this; things seem to be going to rot around me and other supports seem to have crumbled, but this is my God and I am still confessing him.' What a privilege to exercise such defiance!

Or we join in the Disciples' Prayer. I have to admit that I am partial to the last petition: 'Lead us—not into temptation, but deliver us from the evil one' (NIV). Here is a prayer I can pray, I who am so prone to take a 'Lot' approach to life, to look all too superficially at the stuff of life; I need to be kept from being dominated and deceived by the evil one. It is a privilege to seek heaven's protection.

But not all our worship is public worship—some of it is family worship or individual worship; and we should be just as diligent about this privilege. I have always found moving that story in *The Shorter Catechism Illustrated*, edited by John Whitecross, that tells of Robert Balmer. Balmer (d. 1844) became a theology professor in the United Secession Church in Scotland, but, like most theology professors, he was once a child. His father died when Robert was ten years old. Robert had been in the habit of bringing the books for family worship to his father each evening in preparation for family worship. On the evening of the day his father died, Robert brought those books as usual and set them down in front of his mother. This brought an irrepressible outburst of sorrow. But Robert comforted his mother by telling her that God, who had taken away his father, would be a father to them, and that he had promised to hear their prayers. 'And,' he added, 'we must not go to bed tonight without worshiping him.' That is the pilgrim attitude: one simply can't stop worshiping the God who has called him into his marvelous light. That's what pilgrims do—not just within the walls of the sanctuary but around the kitchen tables of their homes.

Covenant people must be careful to remain pilgrims—distrusting appearances and holding on to promises.

4

COVENANT MAN GOES INTERNATIONAL

(Genesis 14)

Theodore Roosevelt seemed to be the center of attention wherever he was. He seemed—from what we're told—full of vim, vigor, and vitality. 'Gusto' was his trademark. Once a citizen begged TR not to allow his fighting spirit to drag the United States into war. Roosevelt replied that there was no way he'd allow a war while he was 'cooped up' in the White House. His daughter Alice once said that her father wanted to be the bride at every wedding and the corpse at every funeral. He loved to have the world spin around him—and often that seems to have been the case. Abraham was like Teddy Roosevelt in that he became the center of attention in Genesis 14 but unlike him in that he did not seek that attention. Here international politics came to Abram; he was thrust upon the world stage; but it was not something Abram was aching for. Yet we can say that in Genesis 14, covenant man (at least Abram will be 'covenant man' after Genesis 15) goes international. But the question for us is: What are we meant to take away from this strange account? I would propose that here in Genesis 14

Abraham's seed are meant to receive both encouragement and admonition for their life in this world.

First, the encouragement. Notice **the special attention God's servant receives** in verses 1-16. And in these verses we find a clip of world politics (vv. 1-12) and a case of daring rescue (vv. 13-16).

Let us focus on verses 1-12 for a moment. Many think this is a very old account, and I would agree with them. Observe how old names are updated for a later readership: for example, Bela is 'now' Zoar (v. 2), the Valley of Siddim is the Salt (i.e., Dead) Sea (v. 3), En-mishpat is Kadesh (v. 7) and so on (see too verse 17). We have no explicit confirmation in details, but names like Arioch and Tidal fit the second millennium B.C., the geography makes sense (this is clearly not Peter Pan stuff), and, yes, kings from Mesopotamia really did carry off expeditions to the west like this (cf. K. A. Kitchen, *On the Reliability of the Old Testament*, 318-23).

It was a revolt by Sodom and her sister cities (the five kings of verse 2) that started everything off. After twelve years of vassalage they revolted and, once the news got back, the four-king alliance led by Chedorlaomer (vv. 1, 5) came to suppress the revolt. Sodom and her sister towns may have been located around the southern end of the Dead Sea. Chedorlaomer and Co. likely came down the Transjordanian highway through the area east of the Jordan where they took out three opposing groups (v. 5), went past the Dead Sea area down to Seir, where they defeated Horites (v. 6), then turned northwest to arrive at Kadesh and trounce Amalekites (v. 7a), and then moved east and a little north to Hazezon-tamar, where they repulsed Amorites and closed in on Sodom and her confederates (v. 7b). (Analogies may not help, but if Chedorlaomer's group came to England, and Oxford, let's say, was where the Sodom group of towns was located, it would be as if the four kings would come down from Northampton to Reading and on to Southampton, then turn northwest to Bath, before proceeding to Swindon and on to Oxford). I am only guessing, but it may be that Chedorlaomer's army neutralized all these subsidiary groups in order to isolate Sodom and her confederates—there would be no one available to give the Sodom coalition any assistance or to strike Chedorlaomer's troops in the flanks or rear. In any event, verses 10-12 suggest that mopping up Sodom's forces was not difficult. As a side note, the tar pits may have been a refuge for the kings of Sodom and Gomorrah rather than the end of them. The verb translated 'fell' can carry the idea of 'let themselves down'; hence they may have 'hidden out' in the tar pits to avoid capture. Naturally, they would need a shower after that.

One might wonder why these four kings would even want to bother to come all this way for what seems a rather inconsequential revolt. Of course, we cannot be certain, but the south end of the Dead Sea was a chief source of copper, the primary metal for making agricultural tools and weapons as well. And Mesopotamia had almost no metal ores and so had to get them from outside—from far-flung cities that they might keep under tribute to them (see Alfred Hoerth, *Archaeology and the Old Testament*, 96). But the real 'kicker' was that Lot was carted off (v. 12), and so, when he finds out about that, Abram feels compelled to attempt a rescue and so comes on the 'world stage.'

So now let us try to get a grip on the setting. Here are the newsmakers of the era (vv. 1-2), the *Time* magazine 'Man of the Year' types, strutting their stuff and their armies on the big international scene; but all this is *subsidiary* to the real center of interest, Abram (v. 14). The only reason Chedorlaomer, for example, makes the Bible record is because of Abram!

This is not our usual viewpoint. We tend to have the 'Today Show' mentality. We hope we get on camera for a split second, on that big national, early-morning TV show. We're hollering out where we're from, waving a sign that says 'Columbia, SC,' and doing a starving-for-attention dance on a cold and wet New York City street outside a major television studio. Maybe, we think, the camera will pan our way and show us frantically waving.

Now that is not the view of the text here. Abram is not mentioned here in order to fit him in among the real movers and shakers, the international 'set' of the day. This text does *not* mean to say, 'You see how Abram appeared in the big time once very briefly?' No, no, that is all wrong. No, Chedorlaomer and Co. only appear because *they* happen to be a mere episode in the big story of Abraham. To oversimplify (and distort) a bit: you have world history and significant history, and the latter revolves around the people of God, that is, Abraham's seed. They are the 'main show' and the head knockers of this age are simply background for this show. I want you to get a taste of this in other—and more familiar—Bible passages.

Remember Luke 2:1-4a? *Now it came about in those days that a decree went out from Caesar Augustus that all the world should be enrolled. This enrollment was before that made when Quirinius was governor of Syria. And all were going to be enrolled, each to his own town. And Joseph also went up from Galilee, from the town of Nazareth, into Judea, to the town of David...* (drawing on Nigel Turner for verse 2). Will Durant tells us that at Augustus' death the Roman empire took in 3,340,000 square miles. He tells us that when Augustus visited Greek Asia in 21 B.C. he was hailed in dedications and orations as 'Savior,' 'Bringer of good tidings,' and 'God the Son of God.' Yet Caesar and his decree are mere background for the real story. And what is that? It's about a carpenter from Nazareth who takes his intended along to Bethlehem and about her first-born son and his feeding trough. Caesar is only a backdrop. Luke 3:1-2 borders on the hilarious; let's set it out clause by clause:

Now in the 15th year of the reign of Tiberius Caesar,
Pontius Pilate being governor of Judea,
Herod being tetrarch of Galilee,
His brother Philip tetrarch of Iturea and the region of
    Trachonitis,
and Lysanias tetrarch of Abilene,
Annas and Caiaphas being high priests,
the word of God came to John the son of Zecharias in
    the wilderness…

For six clauses Luke builds up expectancy, as he pulls up the movers and shakers of the times, who dominate the headlines and get the interviews and fill the tabloids. But they are all a mere prelude to the main and most significant event of the day: the word of God came to John.

We must then get this 'corrected' view, this Bible view that understands that the premier folks of this age are not that earth-shaking. We need a bit of the healthy cynicism of that lady in Macon, Georgia, who once called up her congressman, Bill Stucky, to complain that her garbage had not been picked up. Stucky was a bit miffed that she bothered him about it, so he asked her why she didn't look up the number of her local sanitation department and call there. Back came the replay: 'Well, congressman, quite frankly I didn't want to go up that high!' (Paul Boller, *Congressional Anecdotes*).

Put in right perspective, Chedorlaomer and Amraphel and Washington D. C. and Putin and Beijing and the Pentagon and the United Nations are merely the background of history. God's premier attention is ever on Abraham's family. They are not swallowed up in politics, lost amid scandals, or smothered under the helpless diplomacies and summits of governments and nations. Though they don't make *People* magazine or the evening news, God's mind and his story always seem focused on wherever his people are. So what matters is what happens among Abram's family. What counts is when a father who belongs to Abram's seed sits down on the edge of his eight-year-old's bed, goes over a Shorter Catechism question and answer with him, illustrates and explains the answer, and then prays with the lad before he puts him to bed. What matters is when two or three of Abram's daughters meet together in one of their kitchens in order to intercede for friends and neighbors—or when a Christian turns in a solid day's work. What's significant is when one of Abram's sons spends twenty hours studying and agonizing over a biblical text and then on Sunday morning stands up and preaches it to thirty-five people—or when a Christian mother spanks her four-year-old for disobedience and then, a few moments later, takes her on her knee and prays for her. All this we infer from the special attention God's servant receives.

Now we come to the admonition: notice in verses 17-24 **the typical dilemma God's servant faces**. Abram went off with his 318 men, plus those of his allies. There may have been upwards of a thousand men in pursuit of the four victorious kings. It's something like 110 miles from Hebron, Abram's base, to what is later known as Dan in the far north of Canaan—and then another forty or so miles from Dan over to the region of Damascus (see vv. 14-15). Abram divides his troops, strikes at night, drives away the enemy and recovers both Lot and loot. On his return he encounters two different kings, the king of Sodom and the king of Salem (probably = Jerusalem). No sooner is the king of Sodom mentioned (apparently cleaned up after the tar pit) than Melchizedek cuts him off:

> But Melchizedek king of Salem brought forth bread and
>   wine
> —he was priest to God Most High.
> And he blessed him and said:
> 'Blessed be Abram by God Most High,

possessor of heaven and earth;
and blessed be God Most High
who has surrendered your enemies into your hand.'
And he gave him a tenth of everything (vv. 18-20).

Melchizedek is mysterious, but he seems to be a king-priest in Jerusalem, one who held on to the knowledge of the true God in the midst of Canaan's religious and moral cesspool. He blesses Abram and blesses God. Then we meet the arrogance and perhaps the disdain of Sodom's king: 'Give me the persons, and take the possessions for yourself' (v. 21). The king of Sodom is trying to direct matters, trying to bring Abram under his authority and sway. But Abram will have none of it—he has already declared his allegiance in his 'tithe' given to Melchizedek. He rejects vassal status toward Sodom. Abram is not the only one who faces this dilemma. Many of his 'family' still stand (and do so again and again) before Sodom and Salem. They face the question, Where is my sufficiency? In the gifts of Sodom or in the bread and wine of Salem? To whom do you belong? The question of discipleship to Sodom or Salem pops up continually.

Matthew Propp always thought he was Matthew Propp until one day when, we might say, he got the props knocked out from under him. He was applying for work in the New Mexico prison system and had to search out his birth certificate. He discovered that the Propps who had mostly raised him were not Propps but Smileys, that they had run off with him when he was fifteen months old when an adoption procedure fell through. He was actually Anthony Russini, and time was when his biological parents had spent tens of thousands of dollars to try to locate him. And so at twenty-two, I suppose Matthew/Anthony had to decide to whom he belonged.

And if you share Abraham's faith and belong to Abraham's family you will face the same alternatives—and not merely at the beginning of believing life but all along the way. It is simply basic first-commandment stuff—'You shall have no other gods besides me.' Sodom is always out looking for lackeys (not disciples), always making deals. Salem is about a God who, as possessor of heaven and earth, is adequate to give all that is needed. And in the end all that matters is whether you go on clinging to the One who offers you bread and wine.

5

FAITH FACES THE PASSAGE OF TIME

(Genesis 15:1-6)

I recall reading that John Tyler was stunned when he was told that William Henry Harrison had died after a month in office and that he, Tyler, was now President of the United States. He had not yet even received his first salary payment as Vice President, so he was fund-less; he was president yet didn't have enough money to pay for his trip from Williamsburg to Washington to attend his own inauguration! Friends had to float him a loan. One can have what seems a great privilege and yet find real problems with that privilege.

It's something like that when one has and believes in the promises of the living God—one can discover that the 'believing' part can involve severe difficulties. It is a high privilege to have the promises but to go on believing them is not always a piece of cake. Sometimes God has to provide 'crutches' for faith to walk on. This is the concern of this text and it packs good news for God's wobbly people. It tells us that *it is God's way to meet struggling faith with assurance.* Let us trace this theme through Abram's experience here.

Notice, first of all, **the struggle over promise** (vv. 1-3)—and notice that it is the word of God that stirs up the struggle: 'After these things the word of Yahweh came to Abram in a vision, saying, "Fear not, Abram, I am your shield; your reward will be very great"' (v. 1).

'After these things' links chapter 15 to the events of chapter 14. We might wonder why Yahweh would say, 'Fear not.' What was there to fear? Perhaps because of something renounced? In 14:21-23 Abram rejected any bounty from the King of Sodom, and perhaps Yahweh is saying that, though Abram had rejected those riches, he himself would abundantly supply him. Or, there are some who think the 'Fear not' looks back to the threat of Chedorlaomer and his cronies re-tooling and coming back again to take vengeance on Abram. Or the fear could be over something immediate—that he was just now in direct dialogue with no one less than Yahweh himself. Once more, the fear could be over something anticipated—that is, Yahweh knows Abram is struggling over the passage of time without the fulfillment of his promises and his 'Fear not' shows that Yahweh knows Abram's concern and trial over that. At any rate, though we may not know the precise fear Yahweh addresses, Yahweh's 'fear not' is *not* a throwaway line; the very words show that the God of heaven and earth knows that a large chunk of your life and thinking is beset with fears (how well he knows you!). But it is the word or the assurance of God that stirs up Abram's trouble; a word of assurance disturbs his assurance.

Abram's problem is the problem of time (vv. 2-3). Part of verse 2 is very difficult, but we can reasonably translate these verses as: 'Then Abram said, "Lord Yahweh, what will you give me? And I keep on going childless, and the son of Mesheq [gets] my house—he is the Damascus fellow, Eliezer." So Abram said, "See! To me you have not given seed, and behold, a son of my household will inherit me."' This is the first time Abram speaks to God, as recorded in Genesis.

The problem is the passage of time without fulfillment of promises: 'I keep on going childless.' He has the promise but nothing has changed in his circumstances. So the reassurance from God in verse 1 does not sedate Abram but stirs up his complaint. Yahweh had promised to make him 'a great nation' (12:2), had promised to give Canaan to Abram's 'seed' (12:7). But there's no sign of a seed yet. Please note that Abram is not complaining of the lack of earthly comforts—after all, he *had* possessions and wealth. But Yahweh had promised him a seed and through that seed to bring blessing on the nations of the earth (cf. 12:1-3) and apparently Abram wanted to see Yahweh's saving plan get on the charts. As Iain Duguid says, Abram wasn't simply in love with babies or salivating over an Abram Junior with a heart-melting smile (cf. *Living in the Gap between Promise and Reality*). Abram had the promise but nothing had changed—faith faces the passage of time, and that time can be wearing.

But this very struggle over the promise can provide a ray of encouragement. For one thing, it shows the freedom faith has to complain to God. Now let's be clear what we mean by that. I don't mean Abram rants and raves or that he shakes his fist or stomps his foot like some spoiled brat throwing a hissy fit. You can sense his attitude in his address to God: 'Lord Yahweh,' 'Adonai Yahweh.' He has a complaint, he has a question, but he realizes he is a servant and Yahweh is the sovereign; there may be candor but there is also proper respect and submission and a recognition of his place. Calvin's comment in relation to Genesis 15:8 would actually fit nicely right here: *The Lord sometimes concedes to his children that they may freely express any objection which comes into their mind. For he does not act so strictly with them, as not to suffer himself to be questioned.*

And there is something more: the complaint itself may be a sign of faith. I suppose many might think, 'Oh, no, I should "shush" up; surely I ought not to express my quandaries to God.'

But when Abram brings his difficulties over the promise before God it shows that the promises of God really matter to him.

Paul 'Bear' Bryant was the legendary football coach at the University of Alabama, but long before his tenure as coach there he had played for Alabama in his student days. Things were not going very well during the first part of the 1935 season. Among other things, Alabama had lost to Mississippi State and Bryant had cracked his fibula in that game. He had a broken leg and was 'out', it seemed, for the next game. But the next game was the 'big' one with Tennessee. On the Thursday before Saturday's game, the coach told Bryant he wanted him to suit up for the game—to give the team moral support. The night before the game, in the hotel room, the team doctor removed Bryant's cast. And lo! on game day Bryant played, catching a pass for a first down, catching another one and then, when about to be tackled, he laterals the ball to a running back for a touchdown. Alabama went on to win 25-0. Now that wasn't smart, playing on a broken leg. But it was revealing—it showed how much football really mattered to him.

That's what Abram's questionings and complaint show—the promises of God really matter to him. Abram is caught up in these promises; he wants them; they are precious to him; he wants to be sure of them. But God has not shown any substantial fulfillment of them to date, and this bothers Abram. So Abram brings these questions and this bewilderment and impatience and casts it all at Yahweh's feet. *Only faith would do that!* Unbelief spits on promises, only faith struggles over them; unbelief dismisses promises, only faith debates them—with God. This very struggle over God's word is the beginning of assurance.

Secondly, in verses 4-5 we find **the sacrament of assurance**. Yahweh gives Abram a clarification in verse 4—the 'seed' to be given Abram will not be anyone already in his household but will be someone directly fathered by Abram. Then Yahweh gives Abram a confirmation in verse 5. He brings him outside (apparently in this vision, v. 1), tells him to look skyward, and then says, 'Count the stars—if you are able to count them.' That was the visible sign. Then he said, 'That's how many your seed will be.' That was the spoken word, interpreting the sign.

What we have here is a matter of graphics rather than logic. Yahweh seems more concerned right here to *impress* Abram with the promise than simply to express it to him. Most of us acknowledge the difference a picture makes. One can see a recipe in simple printed form. It usually isn't so hard to understand. But one must supply one's own image of what it might look like. When we read the mere printed recipe we are likely to say something like, 'That *sounds* good!' But it's different if one opens up a copy of *Southern Living* magazine and sees a two-page spread of a dish in all its multi-colored, gastronomical glory. There's the recipe printed down in the lower right-hand corner, but there too is the picture of this luscious casserole or scrumptious salad or whatever. It lays hold of your imagination, it makes an impression, which the mere printed recipe could not do. That seems to be what Yahweh is up to with Abram here. The star-gazing, star-counting episode does not constitute a rational argument, but Yahweh seeks to lay hold of the imagination of Abram's faith. It doesn't make the word or promise more certain but more vivid. It's as if God is saying to Abram, 'Here, let me see if I can give you a picture....'

Verse 5 shows us then that God stoops to the weakness of our faith and seeks to impress us with the firmness of his word. Remember G. K. Chesterton's hyperbole: don't believe anything that can't be told in colored pictures. Well, in the star-sign, God is giving Abram a colored picture, a visual aid to assist his faith. Yahweh does not do this to make his promises more sure (how could that ever be done!) but to make you more sure of his promises. He gives you props to support your faith, gives you some crutches on which faith can go on walking.

But one can almost hear the objection voiced. Someone will say that we are New Testament believers and we are beyond this childhood stage, this elementary level of Old Testament faith that needs pictures to stir up assurance. We are far more advanced now and not nearly so 'primitive.' But if that's so, why do you mess with bread and wine? For is not the Lord's Supper Jesus' authorized picture to impress you with his fidelity to you? Will you say you are beyond the need for that? For as you come to the table with your wobbly faith on a Lord's Day, it's as if Jesus is saying to you, 'Here, let me see if I can give you a picture to help you go on believing. You see this bread? Just as this bread sustains your physical being, so too I will always and ever sustain you whatever your circumstances. Do you see that wine? If I went that far for you, if I laid down my life for your most extreme need, will I not go to any length to hold you up in any lesser circumstance?' No, Jesus does not have you count the stars; he has you come to the table. But the 'picture' is meant to have much the same effect in the sacrament of assurance.

Thirdly, I want you to see **the sufficiency of faith** in verse 6. This verse consists of only five words in the Hebrew text. I want to look at it rather pedantically, at least to start with. I want to make some observations on the text before narrowing in on the focus of the text, the character of faith.

First, the observations. Notice the *form* of this text. This verse is not a part of the conversation between Yahweh and Abram; rather, it is a comment by the biblical writer. I know this is obvious but we sometimes glide from verse 5 right into verse 6 without noticing it. Next, let us deal with the *translation* of the verse, especially the verb. The form of the verb shows it should be translated something like 'had believed,' or better, 'remained firm.' Verse 6 does relate to verses 1-5, but it takes in much more ground—it seems to sum up Abram's prevailing attitude from chapter 12 on. Some translations can give the idea that verse 6 only relates to verses 1-5; for example, the NASB translates 'Then he believed…' and leaves the impression that verse 6 is the consequence of verses 1-5. But Hebrew has a verb form that would have been used if verse 6 was to be taken as merely the consequence of verses 1-5. To put it in Anglo-speak, verse 6 does not begin with 'then' but with 'and' (or, 'now'). 'And he remained firm'—though his faith was tried in verses 2-3, Abram was still maintaining the faith he had had from the first (see chapter 12). So this was *not* the initial moment of faith; it was not Abram's 'conversion'; it was another instance of ongoing faith; it sums up his believing stance.

Then notice also the *significance* of this believing position (v. 6b); the verse tells us why this 'believing' is so crucial: 'he counted it [the believing] to him as righteousness.' This verse is sporting some 'firsts.' This verse has the first use of the noun 'righteousness' in the Bible; also the first use of 'count'/'reckon'/'credit' in the Bible, as well as the first occurrence of 'believe' (or 'remain firm'). Some scholars hold that we are not dealing with salvation here because it is not the issue in the context. But we must remember that the context is bigger than verses 1-5; verse 6 is an 'editorial' comment on the significance of Abraham's faith from chapter 12 on—why it is so important. Indeed, verse 6b seems to be a stellar statement of grace, for one reckons or counts or credits something to someone when that person doesn't have it! So this verse tells of God's gracious decision about Abram: he counted that believing attitude to him as righteousness. 'Righteousness' is not something he had in himself, but God counted Abram's faith as what he wanted and gave him right standing with himself.

And…we must not fail to observe that there is an *overflow* to this text. This text has 'sticky stuff' on it; Paul said so when he quoted it in Romans 4:22-24. Paul quotes the last half of verse 6 and then says: 'Now it was not written for his sake alone that it "was counted to him," but for our sake as well, to whom it is going to be counted—to those who believe on the One who raised Jesus our Lord from the dead' (Rom. 4:23-24). This is still the way God puts people right with himself. It brings to mind what someone sent in to *Reader's Digest* a few years ago. A teacher in one of the local elementary schools was showing a copy of the Declaration of Independence to her class. It passed from desk to desk. Finally it came to Luigi, a first-generation American. The lad studied the document reverently, and then, before passing it on, gravely added his own signature. As if to say: this is not merely something for eighteenth century colonists—this is 'for my sake' as well.

Those are, I think, important observations on the text. Let's shift now to the focus of the text—or at least what is our focus right here—the character of faith. As I noted, my preferences in translating the text is to render either 'And he had believed Yahweh' or 'and he remained firm in Yahweh.' This belief, in context of verses 1-5, has to do with faith in Yahweh's promised word. And yet, as Alexander Maclaren once pointed out, it deals not so much with faith in the promise as in the Promiser; if we believe the former, we are really believing the latter. So the object of faith is Yahweh himself. Now you may say, 'That is so simple; so basic; I already know that.' Oh, I'm not so sure you do. You can easily forget that. Take a very general scenario. You may end up facing some dilemma. Have you, might you, sometimes think 'Ah, I will be able to face this because I have adequate faith.' (You are too modest to claim *great* faith perhaps!). But then you are trusting in your faith and not in God. Your 'adequate faith' is idolatry, because it makes God unnecessary. But true faith is leery of trusting faith; it has recourse to the object of faith, to the God who has spoken promises. And there is a practical implication hidden here, especially for believers of an introspective nature: if the object of faith is what matters, then don't be overly worried about faith itself, wondering how much you have, anxious about the 'amount' of faith.

You may have heard about the death of James Garfield, the twentieth United States president, who died in 1881. An assassin shot him. One bullet grazed his right arm and did no real damage; but the other entered the lower back, deflected off a rib, and lodged near the pancreas. After Garfield was removed to the White House he was under the care of a team of surgeons. He underwent three operations, but the real 'kicker' we might say was that the doctors repeatedly probed the wound with bare fingers and unsterilized instruments, a common practice then. But that continual probing led to blood poisoning, the immediate cause of Garfield's death (W. A. DeGregorio, *The Complete Book of U.S. Presidents*). Bible faith does not keep staring at its own navel or poking at itself worrying about what kind of shape it's in. Bible faith looks away from itself to the One who promises and finds rest there.

I remember making a call on a man in the last pastorate I served; he was both parishioner and friend. He had not long before been diagnosed with a condition that would likely 'take him out,' though that threat was not immediate. He had been a Christian for some years, but, in light of the coming degeneration of his health, he wanted to be sure of his ground before the Lord. It was such a privilege to visit with him and for us to be able to talk so plainly and directly about eternal matters. Before I left and prayed with him, I read from John 6, emphasizing verse 37: 'All that the Father gives me will come to me, and the one who comes to me I will never cast away.' He wanted me to write that down—not just the reference, but to write out the whole verse. I looked in the front of my testament and found a blank 'Post-it' note. So I wrote down the verse and the reference and gave it to him. He put it in his wallet and carried it there. When I saw him some time later—he had moved to another town, he still carried that text in his wallet. He didn't do that because a scrap of paper is some kind of magic, but because it was a clear promise of Jesus his Lord—and in leaning on that promise he was leaning on the Promiser. And when you do that, you will often find deeper assurance because, as this passage says, it is God's way to meet struggling faith with assurance.

We give thanks, O Lord, for the trouble you take to help us go on believing. Teach us not to fret over the intensity of our faith, but convince us that even a weak faith may lay hold of a strong Christ. Amen.

6

How do you spell 'assurance'?
(Genesis 15:7-21)

Mike Deaver was in a tailspin. He was in charge of President Reagan's security detail the day John Hinckley tried to assassinate Reagan. Deaver had grabbed one of his colleagues, Jim Brady, and had shoved him into a different position as they were leaving a hotel and moving toward the limo. One of Hinckley's bullets had caught Brady in the head. He would never be the same. Deaver's anguish wouldn't go away, because he, after all, was the one who had put Brady in that position. Deaver's wife suggested he go and talk with the neurosurgeon who had operated on Brady and had saved his life. Deaver dumped his story, telling the doctor the tough time he was having over his responsibility for Brady's condition. The doctor listened and, after Deaver had finished, asked him how tall he was. Five foot nine. The neurosurgeon went on, telling Deaver that Jim Brady was six feet tall, that if he had stayed where he was before Deaver moved him President Reagan would be dead, because Brady took the bullet that would have killed Reagan. Had Deaver been there, the bullet would have gone right over his head and hit Reagan (Peggy Noonan, *When Character Was King*). That didn't restore Jim Brady to perfect health. But that information gave needed perspective and reassurance and Deaver began to recover.

Christians, more often than not, have the same sort of need; they need reassurance, they need to be settled, especially in being able to go on holding on to God's promises. Hence the importance of Genesis 15, for it teaches us that *covenant is God's answer to faith seeking assurance*. In short, c-o-v-e-n-a-n-t is how you spell 'assurance.' Let's consider several observations on Genesis 15:7-21 that help us to see how God nurtures assurance through his covenant.

At the very first we see **how welcome God's covenant is** (vv. 7-10). In verse 7 Yahweh reaffirms the place-promise: 'I am Yahweh who brought you out of Ur of the Chaldeans to give you this land to possess.' In verses 1-6 God assured Abram of the people-promise (the seed); here he assures him of the place-promise, the land, the home. Abram's response, once more, presses for more: 'Lord Yahweh, how will I know that I will possess it?' (v. 8).

How are we to take Abram's response? I doubt that it is doubt! That is, we have just been told that Abram 'remained firm' in faith (v. 6), so it is not likely that verse 8 indicates unbelief. Rather his words show that the promise matters to him and that he *wants* it to prove firm. His question does not indicate faith's weakness but faith's interest, not faith's wavering but faith's longing—for assurance. Let me compare Abram's concern with a quaint, old-fashioned scenario.

Let's say we have a young fellow and a young woman who are coming up on their last year of college or university. Let's say that they have enjoyed a growing relationship that could well become 'serious.' But this summer before their final year he has a job at quite a distance from her home and so they are not able to see one another for several months. And…let's say this takes place before cell phones and e-mail and so they are reduced to writing each other letters in reasonably coherent

English prose. So they eagerly write and receive letters. Then, as sometimes happens, one can become more bold in writing than if in someone's immediate presence, and so he takes the plunge and asks this girl if she will marry him. He has used the M-word. He is anxious for her reply. Soon he has it by return post. After a few usual courtesies, she refers to 'the question' in his last letter. She writes: 'The answer is "Yes!" No, no, it's not! It is "Yes! Yes! Yes!"' He is ecstatic; he writes back and tells her so. But over the days and weeks his enthusiasm gets tempered by realism, a realism he does not feel free to discuss with her in writing—it must wait till he actually sees her again. For after her positive response he had begun to think how she was socially a cut above him, that if she married him, there was a certain level of ease and support that he could not provide and he began to wonder if she had really considered these things before giving her answer. Summer passes, and they are delighted to see each other again. And when they have freedom to talk he raises his concern. Now why does he do that? Does he want her to say, 'Yes, you are right, of course; I gave a snap answer and I didn't really think about all the ramifications,' etc., etc.? No, he wants to hear, 'Oh, I thought about all those matters a long time ago, Silly! They don't make any difference.' His concern is not so much a matter of grave doubt but of necessary assurance. He simply wants some help in knowing that the wonderful dream is really true.

Now it seems to me that that is Abram's position here. And he seems to know exactly what Yahweh is up to! When Yahweh tells him to get a heifer, female goat, and ram (all three years old) plus a turtle-dove and young pigeon (v. 9), Abram seems to know exactly what to do with them—he hacks the large animals down the middle but does not cut up the birds (v. 10). He didn't have to be told what to do with these animals; he knew what they were for—that Yahweh was going to put a covenant in place. This implies that the covenant is intended to assure Abram. Abram already had the promise; but covenant is more. Covenant is what God does when he gets formal about a promise. Covenant is the wrapper God puts around his promise to help you to believe it. Imagine going into a grocery store that had no wrappers on its canned goods. Well, I said, Imagine. At each aisle there is a clerk who knows and will point out to you what it is you want—but the canned vegetables, and so on, are just there in all their silvery and naked tinny glory. You want Del Monte cut green beans. So the clerk points out to you the shelf and the group of cans. Now that would work, I suppose, and, incidentally, create jobs. But you wouldn't care for it. And that's because you feel more sure of what you're getting if you can see the red, green, and blue label on the can with the proper picture of cut green beans. The wrapper really helps.

Now the big point is what this tells us about *God.* He takes the trouble to enter into covenant—he is willing to go to great lengths to help his people go on believing his promises. He knows the struggles faith has in holding on to his promises, so he stoops down and puts 'handles' on his promises.

Paul Boller and Ronald Davis tell of a 1979 movie *The Electric Horseman.* In the movie Jane Fonda is a TV reporter who comes to know an ex-rodeo star (Robert Redford) who travels around on horseback as a pitchman advertising a cereal. At some point they are to kiss. Sydney Pollack was the director and he wanted them to kiss just the way he wanted, so between 9 a.m. on a Tuesday and 6 p.m. on a Wednesday he did forty-eight takes at a cost of $280,000. The film's cost accountant said it would've been cheaper to have Redford kiss the horse! But Pollack would go to any length to get it 'right'—even if it took thirty-three hours and forty-eight takes to get there (*Hollywood Anecdotes*).

God is more tenacious about his people's assurance. He doesn't dismiss your struggles, telling you to 'buzz off' and quit worrying about it. He doesn't berate you, asking why you can't have the bumper-sticker faith some people seem to have: 'God said it; I believe it; that settles it.' No, it's as if he says, 'Here, let's see if a covenant will help—I'll go to any length to help you go on believing.'

Secondly, God provides Abram with more; in verses 13-16 he tells him **how long God's plans take**. I suppose one could say this segment isn't part of the covenant ritual, but it is certainly a part of the covenant revelation. And it proves very necessary. For here Yahweh gives Abram more insight into *how* his plan for Abram's seed will work out, more detail about how he will eventually bring them into the land. And sometimes clarity can go a long way toward providing deeper assurance. Yahweh gives Abram two bits of helpful information.

First, he tells Abram it will be a *long* time before the promise is fulfilled. Note that he mentions 400 years (v. 13b). And in verse 16 Yahweh says that 'a fourth generation will return here.' Apparently here a generation is roughly one hundred years. So Abram's seed will be sojourners and slaves in a land that doesn't belong to them; but then there is really more than that as we look ahead in the Old Testament. In the terms of the covenant (vv. 18-21) the vanquishing of the Jebusites comes up (v. 21). They were not cleared out of Jerusalem until David's time (2 Sam. 5:6-8). So, it would prove to be about 1,000 years before Yahweh's promise was fully fulfilled. This pattern goes against the grain of our expectations; we are always wanting the kingdom of God to appear immediately (Luke 19:11) and much prefer that God march to our microwave time. God will be faithful, but God is not rushed, not in a panic. Which means that a good bit of our covenant living (and waiting) will be pretty routine stuff.

But there's more. God says that it will be a long, *hard* time before the promise is fulfilled (vv. 13b-14). We have already alluded to this. There will be suffering in their future. By analogy, we might point to Acts 14:22, where Barnabas and Paul tell believers in Lystra, Iconium, and Antioch that it is 'through many tribulations' that we 'must' enter the kingdom of God. And the text in Acts says that this was the word they used to 'strengthen' and 'encourage' the believers. Already the same pattern seems slated for the Old Testament people of God. Covenant people are not spared distress but preserved through it. Yahweh will be faithful to his promises but not apart from but *through* suffering.

Now the question: how does all this assure? It assures because it underscores Yahweh's integrity. Yahweh does not hide the problems of time and suffering that will seem to pose roadblocks to his promises. It is as if Yahweh brings up all the threats and hindrances and obstacles and yet says, 'Now all of this will not keep me from proving faithful to you.' But, you see, he has nothing to hide; he is so candid about it all; he covers up nothing.

One can't always say that about people. In his account of the Soviet gulag, Solzhenitsyn tells of the slaughter at Kengir (*c.* 1954). A section of the camp went on strike, refused to work, wanted some relief in their conditions. It appeared that those in charge might be willing to make concessions. This stir went on for, I believe, over a month. Then one morning came a strafe by a plane over the rebellious camp; then the helmeted troops sporting tommy guns and the T-34 tanks. Troops and tank crews had been loosened up with vodka to make them more efficient and uninhibited in wiping out helpless victims. Tanks ran over prisoners, crushed them against walls; those hiding in latrines were raked with bullets. Over seven hundred were disposed of. The security officer who followed the assault wiped out two dozen with his own firearm. Then he went round carefully putting knives in the hands of the fallen corpses. For what? Well, the photographer was coming to take pictures of the 'dead gangsters.' Should anyone complain about the brutality, why, here was the answer—these fellows were armed; we had to use 'excessive force.' It was all a cover-up.

Yahweh never does that. Jesus never does that. You may remember his words in John 16:1: 'I have said all these things to you to keep you from falling away.' What things? Oh, what he had just warned them about in John 15—about how the world's hatred for him will spill over to them. He, like Yahweh here in Genesis 15, hid nothing from his disciples. All the obstacles and difficulties and discouragements are right out in the open. And what on earth does that have to do with assurance. Simply that you can trust a God like that; you can lean on a Savior like that. He doesn't hide the nasty stuff in fine print in an endnote. His candor stirs up your confidence, his frankness feeds your faith.

Thirdly, our passage shows us **how deep God's commitment goes** (vv. 9-12, 17). Abram has hacked in half and set up the slain animals, though he didn't cut up the birds (v. 10) and then from verse 12 on Abram is passive—he is in a deep sleep; apparently what is said and takes place after verse 12 comes in a dream or vision.

Now we haven't space to review the cafeteria of viewpoints on the meaning of this strange ceremony. Hence I will simply lay down what I believe is the most tenable position—that the incident in Jeremiah 34:8-22 is still the most helpful for understanding what is happening here and that the ceremony depicts Yahweh's taking the curse of the covenant upon himself. The incident in Jeremiah 34 is much later than Abraham, but what it depicts is very similar to Genesis 15. The Babylonians were fighting against Jerusalem and apparently in view of the dire situation some of Judah's men had given their Hebrew slaves their freedom. Well, if Jerusalem goes under, what good would it be to have Hebrew slaves anyway? But these men didn't just grant their Hebrew slaves their freedom. They made it official; they entered into a covenant over it. They hacked a calf in two and passed between the two halves of the calf (see Jer. 34:18). By that ceremony they were saying, 'If I prove unfaithful to the promise I have made, may what happened to this calf happen to me,' that is, May I be destroyed as this calf was. The Babylonians then temporarily lifted the siege on Jerusalem and these men began to think they'd done a foolish thing to give their Hebrew slaves their freedom; they may need those slaves after all! So they re-enslaved them. In blatant violation of the covenant they had made. So Yahweh said he would fulfill the covenant curse they had taken—'I will make them like the calf that they cut in two and passed between its parts' (ESV).

That is, in part, what is happening in Genesis 15—Yahweh is passing between the parts. The smoking fire-pot and the flaming torch (v. 17) represent Yahweh—remember Abram is 'out' and a non-participant in verse 12. Yahweh himself takes on the curse of the covenant—'if I am unfaithful to my promise to you (see v. 7), may I be dis-membered and destroyed as these animals have been.' So what took place? Yahweh 'cut a covenant' with Abram (v. 18)—the 'cutting' may have particular reference to the cutting of the animals. What did the covenant give or offer? Simply the same promise (vv. 18b-21) Yahweh had already given (v. 7), just in a bit more elaborate form. What did the covenant depict? Yahweh—as the God who is faithful to the death.

Some seem to object to this view because they think it leads to theological absurdity (and I wouldn't be surprised if the Bible wants to drive us to the edge of that in order to make its point). Someone may say that this is totally impossible—how can an eternal and everlasting God suffer possible destruction? But Yahweh is not trying to construct theological conundrums for Abram here, or for us. He is seeking to *give him a picture* of his steadfastness that will grab Abram on the bare basement floor of his soul. Once more, Yahweh is not so much expressing truth here, but wanting to *impress* truth, which is so crucial for Abram.

J. C. Ryle tells how vivid George Whitefield was in his preaching. He once was comparing the miserable condition of a lost sinner to that of a blind beggar. The night was dark, the road perilous, and the poor man was deserted by his dog as he neared the edge of a precipice. He could only grope his way by using his staff. Whitefield was so graphic in his description that his audience was kept in breathless silence; when at last the fatal step was about to be taken, Lord Chesterfield actually made a rush forward, crying out, 'He is gone! He is gone!' Now Lord Chesterfield was by no means a believer, but he liked to listen to Whitefield preach. So he was there. And sucked into the drama depicted.

That is why Yahweh stoops to this covenant curse ceremony. In living color Yahweh is saying that he would rather destroy himself than prove unfaithful to his people. Genesis 15 packs a remarkable revelation for us: God himself is willing to suffer the curse of the covenant.

But we who stand beneath the cross of Jesus know that there's more. I can't expound, I can only point you to Galatians 3:10-14, especially verse 13: 'Christ redeemed us from the curse of the law, when he became a curse for us....' God was never false to his promise, to his covenant obligation. But **we** have broken the covenant; we have not kept his covenant law (a digest of it is in Exodus 20:1-17) and so the curse of the covenant rests on us. The marvel is that God not only takes the curse of the covenant upon himself should **he** break it (that's Gen. 15), but that in the person of his Son he takes **our** curse for breaking the covenant upon himself and suffers it for us (that's Gal. 3). Jesus is destroyed for our covenant-breaking.

Nothing drives this point home so vividly for me as that anecdote about Dr John 'Rabbi' Duncan in his Hebrew class. It was the winter of 1864 and Dr Duncan was reading part of Isaiah with his senior class. Something in the text brought to mind the cry of Psalm 22:1, 'My God, my God, why hast thou forsaken me?' (KJV). So now here is Rabbi Duncan—he has left his desk, is bent nearly double, and paces up and down in front of the students' benches. One hand holds his handkerchief and snuff-box, the other a huge pinch of snuff, but these are forgotten as he muses on the Lord's suffering for sinners, turning the matter over in his mind, utterly absorbed. Suddenly a flash seems to go through him, his face lights up, his hand goes up, snuff flies everywhere as he turns to his class and pleads with them, 'Ay, ay, d'ye know what it was—dying on the cross, forsaken by His Father—d'ye know what it was? What? What?' These last words were said as if he had received a partial but not complete answer from someone and was trying to drag the whole answer out of a student. Then he answered his own question: 'What? What? It was damnation—and damnation taken *lovingly.*' With that he dropped into his chair, his head straight and stiff, his arms hanging down either side of the chair, his face beaming, tears trickling down his cheeks—then he repeated in a mix between a half-sob and a half-laugh, 'It was *damnation*—and he took it *lovingly*' (A. Moody Stuart, *The Life of John Duncan*). That's where Genesis 15 begins to take you, for it shows you a God who is willing to suffer the curse of the covenant, and ere long we discover that he is even willing to suffer the curse of the covenant for us. You can almost see in Genesis 15 the nail-scarred hands of the covenant God. That's how deep his commitment goes.

7

WHEN GOD HAS THE SLOWS...
(Genesis 16)

It's often been told—about that day in September 1862 when Federal corporal Barton Mitchell found a bulky envelope in the tall grass of their campsite. Confederates had camped there before and a too careless officer left the envelope that contained three cigars with a sheet of paper wrapped around them. That sheet was a copy of General Robert E. Lee's special orders No. 191, delineating how his troops were currently split up and his plans for a march north into Federal territory. The sheet was not a 'plant,' the orders were genuine, and were soon in the hands of the northern commander, George McClellan. If McClellan moved immediately, he could cut up and destroy Lee's army and essentially end the War between the States within days. But 'urgent' and 'immediate' were not in McClellan's dictionary. He tended to have the 'slows.' He knew the meaning of 'cautious' and 'deliberate.' So he didn't take advantage of his advantage; the result was the bloody mess of the Battle of Sharpsburg (or Antietam), more of a draw than a northern victory, and three more years of war. But this is what I find interesting: when Bruce Catton tells this story in *Mr Lincoln's Army* he actually gets exasperated with McClellan.

One thinks a writer will surely be objective and detached and so on. But Catton gets aggravated at McClellan! He asks, Why couldn't the man have taken fire just this once? When you have the slows, you can even drive historians over the edge!

In Genesis 16 you may wonder if God is like George McClellan. Abram and Sarai receive the assurance of the covenant in chapter 15 but that is followed here by the problem of *chronology*. Time goes on and nothing changes. So we have in Genesis 16 this account of one of the fainting fits of Abram and Sarai's faith, in which they fancy that they have a solution for one of God's problems. God seems to have 'the slows,' and maybe they can help. That is the orientation; I simply want to come at the passage via some observations that seem to digest the teaching of the chapter.

First, notice **what a sympathy the Bible has for the dilemmas of God's people** (vv. 1-3). Our chapter begins with a wearing problem—Abram had been in the land ten years (v. 3) and Sarai still had not given him a child (v. 1). This calls to mind 12:4, a previous chronological note—Abram was seventy-five when he had gone forth from Haran. Ten years had passed. No heir. It may have been that after the reassurance of 15:4-5 Abram and Sarai may have thought that at any time in the near future pregnancy would occur. But weeks roll on, become months, and nothing changes. So Sarai judges that it's time for a little human intervention. Such interventions can often prove disastrous.

When I was in high school the teenage fellows in our congregation took up the offering at the morning worship service. For whatever reason, the church leaders had given oversight of this task to one of our friends, Dennis. That was no problem, except that any unbiased observer could tell that the 'authority' of the position had gone to Dennis' head and made him a bit pompous. One Sunday morning we were singing the hymn before the offering. My friend Dave and I were in a sort of overflow alcove. For some reason Dave had an anxiety attack. He nudged me and indicated that Dennis must have forgotten about having ushers down for the offering. It was nearing the end of the hymn and no ushers were coming down when they should. Why I didn't use my sense and tell Dave to allow Dennis to fry in his own swagger, I'll never know. So, quick and efficient lads that we were, Dave, myself, and two other young fellows walked in from the side and piously took our position in front of the communion table to await the offertory prayer. Did I say that the hymn was not *quite* over? And that's when we felt the tremor in the floor as Dennis and his own legion of ushers began coming down the aisle from the rear of the sanctuary. Fortunately, there was a side door near the front that led out into the church parking lot, and we usurping ushers quickly vacated our spot and dashed through it (as told in my *The Word Became Fresh*). We felt we had to 'fix' the problem and we messed it up terribly.

And Sarai apparently considers that she has a 'fix' for the problem of her barrenness. It seemed a plausible proposal: 'Look now, Yahweh has prevented me from giving birth; go in please to my servant girl—perhaps I can be built up from her' (v. 2). This at least shows that the people-aspect of the promise did matter to her. One would think in light of Yahweh's assurance in 15:4 that Abram and Sarai were to have a son, but Sarai must have begun to think that it might mean that it was for Abram and possibly someone else! There was, after all, this other way sanctioned by Near Eastern culture. In some nineteenth century B.C. Assyrian materials there is a provision that if a wife did not produce children for her husband within two years, she herself could buy a slave woman. After that slave woman had given birth to a child, the husband could sell her off wherever he wished (see K. A. Kitchen, *On the Reliability of the Old Testament*, 325). The situation is somewhat similar here.

So they try the Hagar method (vv. 3-4). It is hard sometimes, isn't it, to know whether faith should act or wait? In any case, what is acceptable in culture may be faithless in the purposes of God. That seems to be the case here.

I say that because it appears the writer gives us a most *telling description* of the situation. It seems that the writer is a tad despondent. Two times he tells us that Sarai is 'the wife of Abram' (vv. 1a, 3a); then he mentions the chronological difficulty—the ten-year wait (v. 3b); then, when he notes that she gave Hagar to Abram, he makes a point to call him 'her [Sarai's] husband' (v. 3c). Now we know all that already—we know Sarai is the 'wife of Abram' and that he's 'her husband.' Yes, but this is the writer's way of underscoring the pathos of the whole affair. It's as if you can almost sense the writer's *sadness*. By his use of 'wife' and 'husband' it's as if he is bemoaning that a proper relation is being intruded upon by this new arrangement. He's expressing something of the heart-rending-ness of the whole thing. Does it hurt any less because it was 4,000 years ago? There is nothing clinical at all in his description. And his mention of the chronological difficulty is in order to remind you of the pressures faith was facing. Now his allusion to the passage of time and the pathos with which he describes their 'solution,' suggests our main point: it's as if the Bible has a great sympathy for the dilemmas of God's people.

Sometimes the pressures your faith faces are 'chronological' ones. You might like to be married and raise a family, but marriage doesn't look hopeful, because there are no Christian men or women in the circles you frequent. And time goes on. Even in college or university it can look pretty bleak. You would think that there would be 'live' possibilities in a Christian college or university fellowship. Now I don't know anything about girls. Our family didn't 'do' girls; I don't know much about them. But I have noted over recent years (at least here in the United States) that Christian guys in colleges are hardly prizes to be desired. It is possible, you know, to be both a Christian and a clod—and there are quite a number of Christian fellows who are the latter. Several years ago, my wife and I were in our car ready to leave after attending a wedding. Out into the parking lot came a young couple, who, I believe, were planning to be married soon themselves. He hopped into the driver's side and she went round and got into the passenger's side. He made no effort to go round, open, and hold the door for her. It was as if he assumed she was a competent cow and could find her own stall. I know the so-called 'new woman' doesn't care for such niceties, but it's not that—it's just courtesy, and most young women prize it. If you go to something a cut above a fast food place (because there one can't really hold a booth for a lady!) and you are to be seated at a table, surely a young man could hold the chair for the young lady he's with. The problem with many Christian college fellows today is that they seem to serve as an argument for evolution, for they act as if they just stepped out from under a rock! None of that can be very alluring for Christian women.

I know, I went on a bit of a tangent. But the difference with me is that I *know* when I go on a tangent. But you may long to be married and there seems to be no Christian 'pool.' But then there is that woman in the office staff, who is not a Christian, but is genial and fun and seems like she would be affectionate, and maybe, yes, maybe you could go that direction and maybe if marriage occurred, she would begin to attend worship with you and maybe she'd eventually be converted and… Or there's another 'time' problem: you have a grown child you've spent years praying for, a child brought up in the faith, taught the faith, loved in the faith, but still shows no evidence of faith in Christ. She's in her thirties now, he's in his forties now, and it seems like there is absolutely no sign of the Holy Spirit's work within them. And the chronology moves on. Or you may be suffering from an aggravating physical condition, whether relatively mild or intensely severe, whether recurring from time to time, or simply unrelenting. You have prayed yourself out over it and you have tried what medications you can and relief is marginal, and time goes on, and nothing changes.

And nothing may. But the way the Bible highlights this quandary and the way the writer here so sympathetically describes Sarai's trial tells me that the Bible understands the pressures God's people feel. I remember reading Emile Cailliet's autobiographical piece called *Journey into Light*. He told of how his wife once brought home a French Bible she had obtained and how he squirreled it away and read and read—and realized this was the book he had been looking for. He called it 'the book that understands me.' Exactly. Even though this narrative does not endorse Sarai's recourse, it nevertheless understands her anguish and sympathizes with her in her pressures and disappointment.

Secondly, we see here **what a disappointing people the covenant people are** (focus mostly on verses 4-6). Now you see a picture of what happens when men and women deviate from the marriage pattern set out in 2:24. It looks like the 'Hagar plan' succeeded: 'And he went in to Hagar and she got pregnant' (v. 4a). As if it was just like that! Did Hagar quip at some point, 'It's not all that hard, Sarai!' Hagar is so fertile it may have sickened Sarai. Now all begins to fall apart. There's a spring in Hagar's step now, a strut in her walk, a disdain in her eye. 'Her mistress was looked on with contempt' (v. 4b). Sarai lays into Abram, 'The wrong inflicted on me is your fault!' (v. 5). Oh? I thought he was simply following orders. That word 'wrong'—you've heard it before in TV news reporting. It's the word *hamas*—violence, or wrong or outrage. So Sarai blames Abram. And Abram, take-charge fellow that he is, pulls back his robe, sticks out his hairy chest, and...wimps out (v. 6). He tells Sarai that Hagar is under her jurisdiction and she can do what she wants with her. Sarai treats Hagar so harshly that she runs away (v. 6b). The laws of Ur-Nammu specified that insolent concubines could be dealt with by scouring out their mouths with a quart of salt. We don't know if Sarai tried the saline solution, but she must have laid into Hagar quite severely. What a disappointing people the covenant people are!

Now don't get your psych book out; don't say, 'My, here's a really dysfunctional family situation.' For there is much more. Notice that the writer 'shades' or 'colors in' the story to show how he regards it (see the commentaries by Wenham and Waltke). Go back to verse 2 for a moment where you read, 'And Abram listened to the voice of Sarai.' The only other place this phrasing occurs is in 3:17, where Yahweh accuses Adam of listening to the voice of his wife! Then note verse 3, where we read that 'Sarai...took Hagar...and she gave her to Abram her husband.' That calls to mind 3:6, where Eve took some of the fruit and gave (same two verbs) to her husband. In other words, the shadow of Genesis 3 falls across the page. As if to say, 'Here is another "fall".' Oh, not unique like that of Genesis 3 but generic, more of the same, aping the original. Yes, here in chapter 16 are the shades of the original fall, here again is the sad twistedness that blights and pervades all our relations and circumstances. How often we realize that we have not really moved far away from the tree of the knowledge of good and evil. Even the motivation seems similar; in Genesis 3 the innuendo was that Eve should not be satisfied with the gifts—and therefore with the ways—of God. That is basically what has moved Sarai here.

It is the malcontent that infects us still. There's one of the Puritan prayers in *The Valley of Vision* that picks up on this tragedy. It reads, in part:

O Lord,
My every sense, member, faculty, affection is a snare to me,
I can scarce open my eyes but I envy those above me,
or despise those below....
If I behold beauty it is a bait to lust,
or see deformity, it stirs up loathing and disdain....
Am I comely? What fuel for pride!
Am I deformed? What an occasion for repining!
Am I gifted? I lust after applause!
Am I unlearned? How I despise what I have not!....
Am I inferior? How much I grudge others' pre-eminence!

That is a good place to begin—to grieve over the blight that Genesis 3 has brought upon us. We may live in Genesis 16, but sadly, it is Genesis 3 that explains us there. We ought never to forget.

It reminds me of that story about Professor John Murray. I think he was with several others having dinner one Lord's Day at Pastor Freeman's. The conversation gathered round our human depravity that we have in and from Adam. Murray himself held forth on this topic for some time. And then Mrs Freeman, quite likely teasing a bit (but the teasing was lost on Prof. Murray), said, 'But Mr Murray, we know that you are not as bad as that.' Murray fixed his good eye on Mrs Freeman and said in his sternest voice, 'Mrs Freeman, if you knew what a cesspool of iniquity this vile heart of mine is you would never say such a thing!' That's really where we must come—to see that Genesis 3 doesn't merely shade in Genesis 16 but hovers over our lives and insides as well.

Where ought this to take us? It should bring us to mourn (Matt. 5:4). It is not morbid but healthy to grieve over the evil that clings to us. I find it fascinating that when Yahweh depicts his restored people, he says of them: *And you will loathe yourselves for your iniquities and your abominations*

(Ezek. 36:31 ESV). That text won't charm you if you're into 'feeling good about yourself' or think that you need to cuddle a 'good self-image.' But don't try to sweep Ezekiel 36:31 aside as if it's something more disposable from the Old Testament. No, the context in Ezekiel 36 describes Yahweh's restored people, people to whom he will give a new heart and a new spirit. And then he fleshes out what people who have a new heart and a new spirit will be like—they will loathe themselves for their iniquities and their abominations (v. 31). This *new sadness* is the evidence of a new heart and a new spirit! Yes, we need to do more than mourn—the New Testament speaks also of 'mortifying' sin (cf. Col. 3:5), but it starts with this mourning and loathing ourselves (much as current psychobabble may oppose it); you ought to carry about with you *as a Christian* a proper sadness, a holy despondency, a healthy broken-heartedness over your Adam nature and the ruin it still inflicts.

Thirdly, we are meant to see **what a marvelous God the covenant God is** in verses 7-16. Four times in verses 7-11 the text mentions 'the Angel of Yahweh,' and, as verse 13 implies, he is Yahweh himself in some kind of visible form. He finds Hagar by 'the spring on the road to Shur' (v. 7b). We can't be exactly sure about Shur, but it would seem that Hagar was heading back to Egypt (cf. 1 Sam. 27:8).

We see how marvelous God is in his *mercy*. One senses that mercy in the sheer beauty of the text, 'And the Angel of Yahweh found her by the spring of water in the wilderness' (v. 7a). And, of course, he knows who she is: 'Hagar, Sarai's servant girl…' (v. 8a). But there is more than meets the eye. Bruce Waltke (*Genesis: A Commentary*, 254) points out that this is the only known instance in ancient Near Eastern literature where the deity addresses a woman by name! And an Egyptian servant girl at that. The Angel of Yahweh finds her and he calls her by name—marvelous mercy.

Yet we could also say that God is marvelous in the *direction* he gives (v. 9). If this text had been written in our day and under only human impulse, it would have God saying, 'I absolutely [one must always absolutely use this overly-used adverb] understand how you can feel that way.' But not in Genesis. There is no evading of responsibility. 'Go back to your mistress and place yourself under her harsh treatment.' One could translate it, 'Allow yourself to be afflicted.' You may not think that so 'marvelous' of God, but it is, in a sense, because it is such a contrast to what we tend to hear in our own day. Sometimes the Lord directs us that way, doesn't he? He doesn't mollycoddle us. He doesn't give us relief, but says, 'Go back and stick it out.'

Some years ago *World* magazine carried a clip that underscored this sort of duty. I think it was from Cal Beisner originally. He had compiled one of those lists of significant events during the past year (1988, I believe)—not the kind most folks think of as noteworthy. Here's one of them: 'Vic and Cindy Jones stuck it out for another year in a marriage that's tough at best, disastrous at worst. "It's not easy," Vic said, "But it's the right thing to do." "That's right," Cindy added. "We don't particularly like each other, but we made a promise that we're not about to break. And we figure real love means doing what's right, not just having warm feelings."'

Note too that the Lord is marvelous in his *comfort*. Yahweh speaks of the son Hagar will bear and instructs her to call his name Ishmael ('God hears'), 'for Yahweh has listened to your affliction' (v. 11b). He sounds as if he will be a rowdy fellow, antagonizing and being antagonized, according to verse 12. But here and now for Hagar, his very name carries the deepest comfort—'Yahweh has listened to your affliction.'

And then God is marvelous in his *wonder*: 'So she called the name of Yahweh who was speaking to her, "You are a God of seeing," for she said, "Have I even here seen after the One who sees me?"' (v. 13). 'A God of seeing' could be taken in one of two ways. It could mean 'You are a God I have been able to see (because you have disclosed yourself to me),' or it could mean, 'You are a God who sees (because you have obviously had your eye upon me).' People who don't like to make choices will hold that both might be intended! Part of her words are difficult to translate, but both ideas seem to be in her words: 'Have I even here seen after the One who sees me?' Hagar had made her own contribution to that domestic mess in Abram and Sarai's house, but the Lord still comes after her and finds her and sees her. She was not out of his sight. God's grace doesn't dry up because we are stupid.

Here is a picture of a marvelous God. There is simply something so very attractive about the God who deals with Hagar and I would urge that the Bible likely wants you to feel the 'pull' of this God. I have always liked the way J. C. Ryle summed up the ministry of George Whitefield, the eighteenth century evangelist. Ryle said Whitefield was a man of a 'singularly happy and cheerful spirit.' In illustrating his point Ryle pointed to the testimony of a 'venerable' lady of New York, who, after Whitefield's death, said of him, 'Mr Whitefield was *so cheerful* that it tempted me to become a Christian.' Isn't that delightful? Tempted to become a Christian! And that's what's happening in Genesis 16: here you read of such a marvelous God because the writer wants to tempt you to give yourself to him.

So here we see the messes the people of God make. But into our arrogance and waffling and nastiness comes the God who finds and who hears and who sees. Our case is never hopeless so long as he hears our affliction and sees us in the wilderness.

8

WHAT DOES IT MEAN TO HAVE A COVENANT GOD?
(Genesis 17)

We are on strange ground here. Yahweh says to Abram, 'I will set my covenant between me and you' (v. 2). One doesn't find that sort of thing in the ancient world—there are no 'covenants' between a deity and humans. Only in Israel. Only Yahweh relates to his people by covenant. Only he is willing to commit himself. 'Covenant' is clearly the focus in this chapter; the word occurs thirteen times. The covenant that was inaugurated ('cut') in chapter 15 is confirmed and set in order here in chapter 17. God himself simply dominates the chapter; Yahweh's speeches take up verses 1-8, 9-14, 15-22; then comes Abraham's response in verses 23-27.

Perhaps the best way to get into the chapter is to allow it to answer our question: What does it mean to have a covenant God?

Having a covenant God means having **a God who baffles us with his strange and stubborn ways**; that is, to have a covenant God means you have a mystifying God. Now right off let's note that there is a huge blank between the end of

79

chapter 16 and here at the beginning of chapter 17. It's only a few blank centimeters in your printed Bible, but actually it's far more. At the end of chapter 16 Abram is eighty-six years old; in the first verse of chapter 17 he is ninety-nine. That's thirteen years of which we know nothing—time simply went by. We'll come back to this.

In the meantime all the attention falls on God's repeated and expanded promises in verses 4-8 and 15-22. They are essentially the same promises, though sometimes expanded (e.g., vv. 4b, 16) and clarified (v. 19). But Yahweh underscores these promises, apparently without blushing: Abraham will become a father of a multitude of nations (v. 5), he will be very, very fruitful (v. 6, though there's not a sign of it to date), he will give all the land of Canaan to Abraham and his seed (v. 8, though not a scrap of it to this point). And then Yahweh becomes stubborn about the way these promises are to pan out—the seed will come through Sarah (vv. 15-16, 19, 21) and is to be called Isaac. Ishmael had been the fruit of Sarai and Abram's Deity-Assistance-Plan in chapter 16; he'll be blessed (v. 20), but he's not on the table as far as the covenant is concerned. The seed comes through Sarah— old, barren, disappointed Sarah. God stubbornly insists it will be that way. It's as if Yahweh should add, 'That's my story—and I'm sticking to it.' He takes the hard way and the long way, and it simply baffles us.

Let's go back to that chronological gap of thirteen years between 16:16 and 17:1. Once when I was teaching Old Testament Survey in a Christian college, one of my students was a fellow from a Jewish background. He'd had some exposure to Jewish traditions but apparently had never had to read (as in my class) large chunks of Old Testament narrative text. One day he summed up his impression from the biblical accounts: 'God is never in a hurry.' The unhurriedness of God seems strange—and unwelcome—to us. The passage of time with no noticeable moves toward promise-fulfillment poses a problem for faith; it can wear on faith. We prefer a deity with high blood pressure who is on the move, whose promises are delivered with microwavable instructions.

There is a corollary to this unhurriedness of God and we should take the time to spell it out. It is this: much of covenant living is undramatic and quite ordinary. Think what went on in those years between 16:16 and 17:1. Well, not much divine razzle-dazzle apparently. God wasn't breaking into Abram and Sarai's life with sensational spurts of drama. I suppose they had clan-wide parties, but most of the time was spent over things like getting goat's milk for morning cereal, doing veterinary work, brushing teeth, getting over the flu, settling disputes over water rights. Great swatches of covenant life are like that. It consists of grocery stores and oil changes, of taking inventory and standing at copy machines, of getting allergy shots and going for music lessons and pulling casseroles out of the oven. Which springs the question: *Can you stand the ordinariness of the Christian life?*

There was once a man in one of the congregations my father served who was very eager to go around and attend various 'special meetings' in the area, perhaps held in another church and/or by a visiting evangelist. Sometimes they called these 'revival meetings.' In any case this man said he went round these various meetings in order to stay juiced up in his faith. He had to have that to keep him stirred up. There is something very sad about that—that one must always have religion on steroids. So much of covenant living is ordinary stuff and if we cannot be content with routine days we will run into problems. God seldom sends fireworks, and because the God of the covenant is a bit strange like that you have to ask yourself: Can I be content with placing one foot in front of the other in the daily round?

Secondly, having a covenant God means having **a God who regales us with his premier and precious promises**. All of verses 3-8 and 15-22 rehearse Yahweh's promises, but I want especially to focus on verses 7-8 here, which rehearse the major promises at the heart of the covenant.

In verse 8 we have the promise of *an unfading inheritance*: 'and I shall give to you and to your seed after you the land of your sojournings, all the land of Canaan, for an everlasting possession….' Of course this 'turf' promise looks no more fulfill-able now than it did back in 12:7. But let's try to get to the root of it. This verse is usually taken as merely the promise of real estate for Abraham's family and descendants. But this verse is a bit different than 12:7. There the promise was: 'To your seed I will give this land.' But here in 17:8 it is 'to you and to your seed after you.' Still this text is usually taken to mean something like the land will be Abraham's in the sense that it will eventually belong to his descendants. But note that the same phrasing occurs up in verse 7: 'to be God to you, and to your seed after you.' No one that I'm aware of dreams of interpreting verse 7 in the 'big glob' way, that is, that Yahweh will be Abraham's God in the sense that he will simply be the God of his descendants. No, we understand Yahweh as promising to be God to Abraham individually and to his seed after him. When therefore the same phrasing occurs in verse 8 ('to you and to your seed after you'), what gives anyone the right to change the rules and take it differently than in verse 7? No, it means the land is promised to Abraham individually and then to his future seed.

This way of taking verse 8, however, poses a conundrum, for Abraham had already been told that he would die without seeing his seed (let alone himself) inherit the land (15:13-15). So…if Abraham himself (note the 'to you' of verse 8) is to enjoy the land, how will that be? It must be post-death, and so there is an implicit argument here for the resurrection of the dead. This really shouldn't surprise us; Hebrews 11:16 has told us that Abraham and Co. desired a 'better country, that is, a heavenly one.' Don't let that send you off in the wrong direction; 'heavenly' doesn't mean immaterial; it does not connote vapor or ether or 'Cool Whip.' (I take 'heavenly' as indicating source in Hebrews 11:16). If the land is promised not just to Abraham's seed but to Abraham personally, and if he is told he will die before either he or his seed enjoy it as a possession, then would he not assume that he must be brought back to life to enjoy the land? Would not faith lead him to assume a resurrection from the dead? Of course, for Abraham the focus in the promise is on the land of Canaan, but from subsequent Scripture we know that Canaan is a chunk of Near Eastern real estate that is going to be part of a new heavens and new earth (note the 'earthiness')—when Abraham will enjoy his inheritance. The testimony to Abraham and his heirs here seems to be that *death cannot ruin your inheritance.*

There is something so 'anchoring' about that. It all reminds me of a footnote in Cornelius Ryan's book *The Last Battle*, the story of the downfall of Berlin in 1945. In all the chaos and destruction that was afoot in those days Ryan says that two operations went on without a break: the keeping of meteorological records did not miss a day in 1945 and eleven of Berlin's seventeen breweries (involved in 'essential' production according to the government) continued making beer. I'm not high on weather records and don't care a lick for beer, but one has to admire that in a way. There are some things even war and destruction can't stop. Nor can death cancel out the everlasting inheritance of Abraham and his believing seed.

But these promises also involve *an indescribable gift* (especially v. 7b): 'And I shall maintain my covenant…to be God to you, and to your seed after you.' Here I think we can do nothing better than to quote from Donald Macleod:

What did God say to Abraham? 'I will be your God.' What does that mean? It means that God is saying to

Abraham, 'I will be for you. I will exist for you. I will exercise my God-ness for you. I will be committed to you.' There is no way that can be improved upon! There is no more glorious promise: not in Romans, not in Hebrews, not in Revelation, not in the Gospel of John, not in the Upper Room: nowhere! These words of the Abrahamic covenant have never been excelled and never will (*A Faith to Live By*, 251).

We might find a pale, pastel analogy in the traditional marriage ceremony. When the man, for example, promises to be 'your loving and faithful husband,' the rest of the vow fleshes out what that phrase is supposed to mean—'in plenty and in want, in joy and in sorrow, in sickness and in health.' So the husband is promising 'I will be with you and for you in all circumstances and be all that a husband ought to be in them.' (I know—we should swallow hard.)

So, when Yahweh says, 'I will be God to you,' he is pledging to be all that God should and could and would be to his servant; all that God should be and would be he *will* be to his people. Once God says this to you, he establishes 'a caring, protecting relationship which is as permanent as the living God who makes it' (R. T. France, *Matthew*, 318). This is a relation that no time can exhaust, no circumstance can change, no disaster destroy, no catastrophe can crush, that no human abandonment can alter. When Yahweh says, 'I will be God to you,' you have the world!

So what? If we have these promises what should we do? Develop a Simeon Lee syndrome. In *Hercule Poirot's Christmas*, one of Agatha Christie's murder mysteries, she relates how Simeon Lee used to go to his wall safe where he had stashed a bunch of uncut diamonds that he had gotten from South Africa. Lee would open the safe, pick up handfuls of the diamonds and let them run through his fingers—for the sheer pleasure of feeling them. That is the task for a covenant believer—repeatedly pick up Yahweh's promises and let them run through and over one's mind for the sheer pleasure of feeling their power and assurance.

Then, thirdly, having a covenant God means having **a God who expects enthusiastic embracing of his covenant** (vv. 9-14, 23-27). Now the 'I' (or 'me') of verse 4 is matched by the 'you' of verse 9—Yahweh expects a response to his promises. God told Abraham to be 'whole-hearted' in verse 1, and Abraham shows that he is whole-hearted by his immediate obedience in verses 23-27. You might imagine his putting out the call: 'Hey, all you fellas, bring all your lads, come to that big tent with the big red 'C' on it—we've got some minor surgery on tap!' You may recall that in chapter 14 Abraham had 318 men in his attack force, so there could easily be over 400 here, possibly a good many more than that. It was minor surgery but a major operation to cover the whole camp. Who knows if they could do it in one day, but they at least started.

First, let's deal in a few details. Yahweh demanded that all the males in Abraham's entourage be circumcised, 'circumcised in the flesh of your [plural] foreskin, and it shall serve as a sign of the covenant between me and you [plural]' (v. 11). Circumcision was the cutting away of the foreskin on the male sexual organ. This applied to all males, whether a male born in Abraham's household or a male who may have been purchased from outside. (The second person 'your' fluctuates in verses 12-13 between singular and plural, since the practice will prevail beyond Abraham's own time and will involve following generations). The 'normal' candidate will be newly born male babies—they are to be circumcised on the eighth day after birth (v. 12a). This circumcision will serve as a 'sign of the covenant' between Yahweh and Abraham's people (v. 11b), so that, as Yahweh says, 'my covenant shall be in your flesh as an everlasting covenant.' It seems that circumcision is God's 'brand,' marking one out as belonging to the covenant and pledged to the covenant God.

Circumcision was widely practiced among other peoples in the Near East, but usually as a puberty or pre-marriage rite. Only in Israel was it performed on the eighth day after birth. And there were other peoples who practiced both male and female circumcision, but in Israel only males were circumcised. Not that females were excluded from the covenant but it seems that they were 'covered' under the sign carried out on males.

What of the significance of circumcision? If it is 'a sign of the covenant' what does it signify? Well, it's hard to get away from the idea that it signifies promises. You note that Yahweh's promises infect the whole context of the circumcision section. That is, verses 9-14 (circumcision) are surrounded with Yahweh's promises (vv. 4-8 and 15-21), promises fore and aft, we might say. Alec Motyer said that whenever Abraham would look upon that sign in his body, he would say, 'I am the man to whom God has made promises.' That is true, and yet this circumcision is also Abraham's *response* to the covenant promises and to Yahweh's command and it would also indicate that he is marked out *for* the God who made the promises—he is 'branded' as belonging to the God who makes promises. Perhaps it's something like a husband's wedding band. On the one hand, he can look at it and say, 'I am the man to whom promises have been made'; on the other, he could say, 'I am marked out as belonging to another.' In this latter sense, Abraham might say, 'I am not my own; I belong to another, for I am branded with the identity mark of the covenant God.'

Christians disagree among themselves when they begin to make inferences about how this covenant 'sign' carries over into our practice now. (I have no desire to be nasty and yet I see no reason to tip-toe around the matter; since this is a sermon I will continue to develop this point as I would among our own congregation, and if the reader is of a 'baptistic' persuasion, he or she may want to cease reading and go to the next chapter.) But you note that eight days after birth was the norm for circumcision. Why didn't Abraham dispute this? Why not ask the Lord, 'Are you sure about this? Wouldn't it be better to let it go until he understood something about it? I mean, he'll cry, and all that, but he won't have a clue what it's all about.' Or what if Abraham had spouted some nonsense like, 'But shouldn't he be allowed to choose for himself?'

This congregation (see note above) stands among those believers who hold that, though the covenant sign has changed in the New Testament era, the covenant pattern has not and that therefore children of covenant believers are to receive the sign of the covenant, baptism. You may ask, 'You mean they don't have a choice?' No, they don't; their believing parents see that they are marked out to belong to the covenant God from the first. Now if you are a Christian parent, I hope you use your child's baptism for in-house evangelism. You may do that different ways. You might make a point to celebrate your child's baptism day each year. Take him or her out for lunch and conversation. The conversation involves speaking at age-appropriate levels about what his baptism involves. What does water represent? What is baptism meant to tell you about your need? You can speak of how such a sign marks one out to belong to the covenant God.

At some point, perhaps at a little older age, you might show him a copy of the vows you and your wife took at his baptism, asking him why parents would say such things, make such promises. Perhaps when he is still older there may come time for a warning note, for it's not strictly true that he has no choice. In Abraham's day a man had a choice (v. 14)—he could reject circumcision, which meant he rejected the covenant and the covenant God. It meant that man did not care about the promises and repudiated any connection with the God who made them. And he would be cut off by God. And so the day may come when you will need to plead with your teenager: 'Now we placed that sign on you to belong to our God, but you can repudiate this covenant, you can say you want no part in it—and perish.' It may be what that child needs to hear at such a time.

In any case, you should welcome the covenant sign (whether your baptism was prospective as an infant or retrospective as a believer), for it marks you out, it claims you, just as circumcision signified in Genesis 17. In fact, the baptism 'formula' in Matthew 28:19, 'baptizing them into the name of…' (literally) is banking or accounting terminology pointing to a transfer of ownership. So your baptism says, 'I am not my own; I belong to Another, and I rejoice in it.' What can be so delightful as to end up in the clutches of the covenant?

9

FAITH FACES THE FACTS OF LIFE
(Genesis 18:1-15)

In one of Gary Larson's 'Far Side' cartoons there are two miniscule spiders on a sidebar at the bottom of a sliding board on a children's playground. They have just woven a giant web across the bottom of the sliding board. One spider says to the other, 'If we pull this off, we'll eat like kings.' But, of course, they need to face the facts of life—no way that will happen. And, if we only take a 'flat-footed' view of the situation in Genesis 18, we'd say the same thing about it. Abraham's visitor lays down his assurance in verse 10: 'I will certainly return to you next year and—indeed!—Sarah your wife will have a son.' But verse 11 tells the 'facts': 'and Sarah was long past menopause.' Such an assurance then was enough to make one laugh—and Sarah did (v. 12a). It was all as likely as Gary Larson's spiders eating like kings.

But we're getting ahead of ourselves, and, actually, slightly off track since we're looking only at the human problem rather than viewing the text the way it wants to be viewed—with the focus on God (cf. v. 1, 'Yahweh appeared…'). If we look at it that way, the text seems to be saying that *the covenant Lord is the one who both draws near and disturbs*. We'll look at the passage in light of that double emphasis.

First, in verses 1-8 we meet with **the friendship of the Lord**. The text tells us that precisely at the time one wanted to doze off—the 'heat of the day'—Abraham had visitors (v. 1b). Suddenly in that drowsy afternoon everything kicks into high gear as Abraham 'ran from the tent opening to meet them' (v. 2), begs their permission to lavish hospitality (vv. 3-5), and, receiving such, bursts into a flurry of activity. 'Abraham dashed into the tent to Sarah. "Quick…, three measures of fine flour! Knead it and make loaves!"' (v. 6). A bit abrupt to one's wife! And twenty quarts of flour! Off he runs to the herd (v. 7) and arranges for a whole calf to be butchered. And all this will be what Abraham called 'a bit of food' in verse 5! But Abraham evidently looked on the opportunity to sustain these guests as a providential privilege (cf. verse 5b: 'for this is the reason you have passed by your servant'). Finally, by the middle of verse 8, after several hours of preparation, Abraham is able to relax as they eat. One can almost imagine his saying, like some waiter in a western restaurant, 'My name is Abraham, and I'll be taking care of you today.' There is no doubt about the identity of at least one of Abraham's visitors, for verse 1 clearly tells us that 'Yahweh appeared to him'; however, Abraham's perception of his identity may have taken some time to develop—it could be that Abraham's 'My lord' in verse 3 is somewhat equivalent to 'Sir.'

That is the text. But what is the testimony in this text—or the insinuation of the text, if you like? It seems to be telling us that there is both a mystery here and a marvel here. It is showing us that Yahweh apparently delights to meet with his servant. Robert Candlish has pointed out something interesting about Yahweh's meeting with Abraham. He said that when Yahweh appeared to Gideon and to Mr and Mrs Manoah (in Judges 6 and 13 respectively) they brought out food and drink, but Yahweh turned it into a sacrifice. But it is different with Abraham. Here he personally accepts Abraham's hospitality, partakes of his provision, sits under his tree, and eats a meal. As S. G. DeGraaf puts it: there was the Lord, the God of heaven and earth, eating at the table of his servant. So Abraham really is Yahweh's friend (2 Chron. 20:7; Isa. 41:8)! The Lord is not 'distant' but loves to be near his people. He is the sociable God; he is awesome but not 'stuffy'; he is the Lord who draws near.

In a book on preaching David Larsen wrote that we don't always realize how we come across to other people. He said that the president of Dartmouth had been accused of having a critical, impersonal style. So he asked his daughter, 'Susan, do you think I'm cold, aloof, and non-communicative?' Her revealing response was: 'Oh no, Mr President.'

But that is not Yahweh's way, that is not his tendency. Living as we do in post-John 1-time, when 'the Word became flesh' (John 1:14), we know that our God is not aloof. Indeed Jesus said—in part to encourage his disciples, 'If any one loves me, he will keep my word, and my Father will love him, and we will come to him and make our home with him' (John 14:23). Nothing distant there. And you find the same tendency in Jesus' words in Revelation 3:20. No, I don't mean that you should expect a divine visit under a tree—primarily because we no longer need that. We have no need of intensely personal revelation, for redemption has been accomplished and we have a full written revelation in Scripture and we enjoy the 'means of grace' in our congregations (the word and sacraments). But all of these 'situational differences' don't change the nature of our God, for Genesis 18 still shows us what is so very *typical* of Yahweh—how he comes near to offer the friendship of the Lord! Indeed, this is how he so often discloses himself to us in those 'standard' means of grace. I think of what Andrew Bonar once said to his people at a Lord's supper celebration: 'Jesus is walking today among the seven golden candlesticks, and he will stop here, at our Communion Table, to see if any of you want anything from Him.' That is the friendship of the Lord.

But the covenant Lord not only draws near—he also disturbs, and that brings us, secondly, to consider **the foolishness of the Lord** (vv. 9-15).

Time for the after-dinner conversation, and a fascinating conversation it is. How did Abraham's Visitor know the name of Abraham's wife? And there's that graphic touch of Sarah hiding behind the tent flap with ears bent to hear (v. 10b)! She was, the text says, 'behind him,' that is, behind the Visitor. If so, how did he know that Sarah laughed (v. 13) when he had reaffirmed his promise (v. 10)? The writer doesn't tell us—he wants us to think about it and figure it out. The promise in verse 10 ('I will certainly return to you next year and—indeed!—Sarah your wife will have a son') is a re-affirmation of what Yahweh had told Abraham in 17:16, 19, and 21. But maybe Abraham hadn't told Sarah, and maybe that's why the assurance here in verse 10 may have caught her by surprise. We're loath to think Abraham may not have told her. We love to assume that the two must have had a long-standing, candid, trusting, ideal relationship in which there were no secrets, and so on. But perhaps Abraham thought these more recent and definite assurances would be painful for Sarah, might tug open a wound. In any case, when Sarah heard it here, it seemed to stretch credibility to the snapping point (v. 12). All of which brought on Yahweh's marvelous question-statement in verse 14: 'Is anything too wonderful for Yahweh? At the appointed time I will return to you next year, and Sarah will have a son!' Sarah felt so trapped, she fibbed (v. 15). But Yahweh is insisting on 'doing it' in his own impossible way; verse 14 is the testimony of the Lord's 'foolishness.'

Now we need a little clarification about verse 14, about how we are to understand it and use it. Here the 'people-promise,' the seed-promise, is honed to precision at last, right down to the who and the when. And verse 14a ('Is anything too wonderful for Yahweh?') mainly relates to that. But we can scarcely read it without getting an itch to apply it in our own circumstances.

And we can—provided we use it with the meaning it has here in its original context. Verse 14 does not teach or suggest that God will do anything incredible for you if you simply exercise enough possibility thinking (i.e., close your eyes tightly, fold your hands, and vanish negative thoughts), but it teaches that God will do *what he has promised* though it seems incredible. The question is tied to a promise. And we must use it that way. And we do have incredible promises. We have the promise of forgiveness (Eph. 1:7; cf. Mark 2:5). Doesn't that seem too wild to be true? Or we have the promise of life; Jesus says to us, 'The one who believes in me shall live even though he dies, and whoever lives and believes in me will never, ever die' (John 11:25-26). That's right up there with a ninety-year-old post-menopausal woman giving birth to a son! Or we have the promise of security: 'All that the Father gives me will come to me, and the one who comes to me I will never cast out' (John 6:37). How can we be so sure of that? Well, is anything too supernatural (really a synonym for 'wonderful' in our text) for Jesus? So when we apply verse 14a to our circumstances we must be sure we are connecting it with God's promises; otherwise we are perverting the text.

But let's try to press on for a bit more explanation. Why does the Lord sometimes insist on doing things this way? Answer: Because he wants to show that what is done can only be his work. Imagine a four or five-year-old lad who wants to 'help' his father rake leaves. His dad gives him a rake and the kid maybe contributes a little. Or he wants to help his dad wash the car. The father would get it done more quickly without such help. But he takes the time to show his son how to wash the parts he can reach and how to rinse each with the hose after he washes it. He gets to 'help.' But when the father has to go up on the roof of the house to put roof 'goop' around a vent pipe, the law is laid down: you cannot help; this is dad's work; you cannot contribute this time; you can stay down on the ground and cry if you want, but this work is not for you.

It always reminds me of that classic 'Peanuts' cartoon strip. Charlie Brown is walking across an iced-up pond, his feet go out from under him, and he ends up flat on his back. Trouble is he has wrapped himself up in so many warm clothes that he cannot bend enough to get any leverage in order to get up. At last reason and despair lead him to conclude that he will never get home, he will have to lie there till he freezes to death. Then dog Snoopy appears and looks knowingly at horizontal Charlie. Snoopy then goes behind Charlie, puts his head down and, having no traction problems, pushes against Charlie's head and slides him off the ice—apparently the most embarrassing thing that had ever happened to the rescued.

Sometimes God insists on that—on using our helplessness to highlight his power. And you might notice that Genesis 18:14 re-appears in the New Testament in an analogous situation. You may not think of it right away when you read Luke 1:37, but it's really alluding to Genesis 18:14. Only this time the birth is not to come from a post-menopausal ninety-year-old but from a virgin teenage girl. God leaves his signature on his redemption-plan by bringing it about through huge 'impossibilities'—through a menopausal woman at the first and through a virgin who conceives at the last. We are meant to conclude, 'Only God could do that.'

It seems to me that we can draw certain implications when God gives overwhelming evidence that his redemptive scheme is his supernatural work. If Yahweh began a people in an impossibility (Sarah bearing a son), then that people can never be eradicated; and if God brought a redeemer of God's elect into the world through an impossibility (Mary bears Jesus), then the redemption he achieves can never be undone or reversed. It seems that the foolishness of the Lord gives us a firm place to stand.

So there you have it. His friendship for you to enjoy; his foolishness for you to adore.

10

Standing before the Lord
(Genesis 18:16-33)

No one talks about Sarah Polk anymore. Maybe she lived too long ago. She was the wife of the eleventh United States president, James K. Polk, and she was by all accounts a 'formidable woman.' She was bright, lively, well-read and well-spoken, and drew complaints from women because she preferred the men's parlor (and political discussion) to the ladies' sitting room (and small talk). She did not upstage her husband but always sought to support him. She had long served as his private secretary (even after he became president), looked over newspapers for him and briefed him on books, discussed leading current events with him, informed him of political developments when he was out of town. She was the only person Polk completely trusted. All during Polk's tenure (1845–49)— and before, she was his 'right hand woman' (Paul F. Boller, Jr, *Presidential Wives*). Her position brought her both important privileges and duties.

That's the way it is with Abraham in our text. Yahweh had placed him in a special capacity. The visitors are heading off toward Sodom (v. 16) and Yahweh engages in a bit of self-talk (vv. 17-19) in which he asks if he should keep Abraham in the dark about his plans in view of Abraham's 'importance'—he is to become the channel of blessing to the nations (v. 18) and the head of a righteousness-doing body of descendants (v. 19). In view of his special capacity he should be taken into Yahweh's special confidence—and therefore be given an opportunity for intercession (cf. vv. 20-21) in which he can explore the justice and mercy of the Lord. Of course, we are not Abraham, but if we are his 'clones' by faith (cf. Gal 3:7), then will we not find that we too have, in our own orbits, a similar privilege and responsibility of 'standing before Yahweh' as he did—and therefore have need of the teaching of this text? We will develop this teaching by means of certain key words.

The first word is **invitation**, and this shows us **how God entices us to prayer** (vv. 20-22). In verse 20 Yahweh summarizes the 'report' ('The outcry of Sodom and Gomorrah—how great it is! And their sin—how very severe!') and in verse 21 tells of his intended 'investigation' ('I mean to go down and see whether they have completely acted in line with its outcry that is coming to me; and if not, I will know'). The word 'outcry' alludes to the wrong and injustice prevailing in these cities that 'cries out' to be righted, for God's judgment to deal with the wrong. Don't let the 'human' language of verse 21 throw you off (as if the all-knowing God had to gather data)—it is saying that whatever God does will not be some 'knee-jerk' reaction; it will be based on a thorough and accurate knowledge of the situation. Perhaps we may paraphrase: in verses 20-21 it is as if God is saying to Abraham, 'This is what's going on.' And Abraham takes the 'bait' (v. 22).

What do I mean by 'bait'? Well, it seems to me that the statements in verses 20-21 have glue all over them. These verses don't merely communicate information but act as an invitation. It's as if the Lord is saying to Abraham, 'Now please talk to me about this situation.' And he does (v. 22): 'Abraham went on standing before Yahweh.'

All this may bring to mind a later sample of the same thing. In Exodus 32 Israel had committed apostasy right in the shadow of Sinai, worshiping a bull image. Up on the mountain Yahweh informed Moses of this, and said: 'I have seen this people, and, indeed, it's a stiff-necked people; and now, leave me alone and let my anger burn against them, that I might finish them off, and I will make you into a great nation' (Exod. 32:9-10). What is Moses to say? 'My sentiments exactly! I'm tired of them too! Let's get on with it!' No, Yahweh wanted Moses to respond in the way he did; Yahweh wanted to stir Moses to arduous intercession for Israel (see Exod. 32:11ff.). Of course, there will always be some who object to Yahweh's technique and perhaps accuse him of being devious. But why can't the God of heaven be at least as sophisticated as we are? We sometimes don't use a direct approach; we may state something with the intent of drawing out a certain response. That was Yahweh's way with Moses. Yahweh's 'intention' in Exodus 32:9-10 was actually an invitation, which in turn stirred Moses to a gut-wrenching process of intercession (see the rest of Exodus 32 all the way to 34:9). One might say that Yahweh *tempted* Abraham and Moses to prayer.

We are used to this sort of exercise in normal human relationships. One of the more 'upper-crusty' department stores in the American south is called Dillard's. Now suppose a wife says to her husband one sunny Tuesday morning, 'I think I'll go out and look over some clothes at Dillard's.' What is she doing? She is putting out a 'feeler,' she is fishing for a response of some kind. Her statement is not a bare statement. She really won't be satisfied with a grunt. She wants to know if she'll hear, 'Oh my, we can't afford a buying spree right now!', or if she'll hear something like, 'Okay, drive carefully.' The wife's statement is a statement, but it is actually one with a what-do-you-think-about-this tacked on to it. That is God's way with Abraham in verses 20-21. And it tells us that God moves our prayers, that he draws us to pray.

Sometimes this can occur in rather dramatic ways. Mary Morrison was converted during the revival on the Isle of Lewis (1949–52). Duncan Campbell was the premier preacher in that revival. He afterward became principal of the Faith Mission Bible College in Edinburgh, where Mary Morrison also went to train. Sometimes when students, like Mary, went out on missions throughout Scotland, Duncan Campbell might go to preach and work along with them. There was a kind of camaraderie among those who labored together. That as background. In 1957 Duncan Campbell went to South Africa on a preaching tour. He was speaking one afternoon and evening in Pretoria—and a great burden for him came over Mary Morrison back in Britain. She went off by herself and prayed for him. Then she immediately wrote to him, asking if anything was wrong and noting the day and time when she had been so burdened for him. It turned out that at that exact time he had been preaching in Pretoria, in the middle of his message, when he suffered a severe hemorrhage and had to be rushed to hospital right from the platform (Colin and Mary Peckham, *Sounds from Heaven*, 45). Mary Morrison was 6,000 miles away—yet God moved her to pray at just the right time.

But sometimes God's 'nudges' to pray are much more routine. You may receive a note from a friend that asks you, 'Do you know what Alan is facing just now?' It may be family trouble or a health breakdown or a faith crisis—whatever. But simply hearing the report and the update makes you conclude that God is calling you to prayer on Alan's behalf. No bells ringing, no dramatic timing that you know of—simply a bit of information that you take to be one of the Lord's invitations to intercession.

Now there is a second word to remember: **Revelation**, and here we need to note that **we come to a God with a known character** (vv. 23-25).

[23]Then Abraham drew near and said, 'Will you really sweep away the righteous along with the wicked? [24]Perhaps there are 50 righteous in the midst of the city—would you really sweep it away and not spare the place for the sake of the 50 righteous in it? [25]Far be it from you! From acting this way—to put to death the righteous along with the wicked, and so the case of the righteous is the same as the wicked. Far be it from you! Shall not the Judge of all the earth do right?'

Note how Abraham's words assume the righteous character of God. John Currid (*A Study Commentary on Genesis*, 1:334) points out that Abraham's prayer is not a request for the reprobate to be saved or that justice should be prevented; rather, 'it is an intercession on behalf of the elect, that God would spare the believers in the city.' Abraham is pressing for what is righteous in this situation, and as he does so he assumes he is dealing with a righteous God.

A pagan could never assume that. Dealing with pagan deities was like getting a letter from Senator William Allison of Iowa. Once Allison dictated a long letter to his secretary, a letter that was in answer to some pointed questions from a constituent. When he had finished, he asked, 'What do you think of that reply?' His secretary hesitated but politely said, 'To be entirely candid, Senator, it is difficult to gather exactly what you mean.' He was gleeful: 'Admirable! Admirable! That's precisely the idea!' (Boller, *Congressional Anecdotes*).

Now the so-called deities of paganism were like that. Those deities had Attention Deficit Disorder in excelsis; they were utterly capricious; no pagan thought the decrees of the gods had to be just. The gods were morally indifferent. Man was made in order to do the dirty work of a defeated batch of gods. There are pagan prayers that lament that it is impossible to know what the gods want. In paganism one had little idea of what one was dealing with in the case of any particular 'god.'

Now Abraham doesn't have all the answers, but can't you see the pillow he rests upon? 'Shall not the Judge of all the earth do right?' (v. 25b). That is the anchor. Not that Abraham or you won't face mystery; but there is always this fundamental clarity, this bedrock, that at the heart of things stand righteousness and mercy. You can rest a pile of mysteries and dilemmas and even heart-breaks on verse 25b.

A few years back *Leadership* magazine passed on one of Maxie Dunnam's stories. It was about when Lloyd Douglas, author of *The Robe* and other novels, was a university student. He lived in a boarding house. Downstairs on the first floor an elderly and infirm former music teacher lived. They had a daily ritual. Douglas would come down the stairs, open the old man's door, and ask, 'Well, what's the good news?' The gentleman would pick up his tuning fork, tap it on the side of his wheelchair, and say, 'That's middle C! It was middle C yesterday; it will be middle C tomorrow; it will be middle C a thousand years from now. The tenor upstairs sings flat, the piano across the hall is out of tune, but, my friend, *that* is middle C!' In the middle of everything else, there was something solid.

And it was Yahweh's righteous character that anchored Abraham's prayer. I wonder, have you ever had a thanksgiving episode over Yahweh's character? True, there are plenty of perplexities we have with God, but there is this bedrock of his righteous character that gives us a firm place to stand in all our dealings with him. 'Clouds and thick darkness are round about him; righteousness and justice are the foundation of his throne' (Ps. 97:2 RSV).

And then we come to a third word: **Implication**, and this tells us **how the presence of the righteous matters** (vv. 26-33). The presence of the righteous matters because they may prove to be a shield for the wicked from judgment. (You may wonder, of course, who are the 'righteous'? A quick answer comes from Psalm 32: the righteous who are to rejoice [v. 11] are the same as those who trust in Yahweh [v. 10], or—further back in the context—those who have been forgiven of their sin, rebellions, and iniquity [vv. 1-5]).

The descending math of Abraham's prayer (from fifty down to ten) is not a piece of human manipulation. Rather, as Derek Kidner says, Abraham is 'exploring,' feeling his way to see how far mercy might go even in the service of justice. In light of the whole Sodom story, this countdown process underscores Yahweh's justice in destroying Sodom (he would spare it for ten righteous, v. 32, yet he did destroy it since ten such were not found). But the principle operating in and with and behind Abraham's intercession seems to be that *the presence of God's people benefits the wicked in this age*, for the presence of the righteous may hold off or postpone judgment on the wicked. Naturally, it's not likely the wicked will realize this or even care; they only think your standards are too stringent, your beliefs too narrow, your lifestyle too straight, your ethics too outmoded. But…might this be one reason why God's judgment does not come upon nations today as swiftly and completely as it might?

So the living of the righteous matters. Don't ever think that your covenant life lacks importance, that living a godly life in this age does not count. What is a 'godly life?' Well, one of the Titus 2:12 variety, where the grace of God trains us 'to live self-controlled, upright, and godly lives in the present age' (ESV). And what does that mean? In context (Titus 2:1-10) it means to live as older men, older women, younger women, younger men, and slaves who are Christians, are supposed to live. And if you check out that context, you'll find it's all pretty basic, routine stuff. Should anyone ask you why you live as you do, the answer would be, in light of Genesis 18: to give God a reason not to bring judgment on you as soon as he normally would. You may need to explain that—or you can just allow them to scratch their heads for a while.

We rightly hold that an exposition of Scripture should bring a response from us, often that we should *do* something because of what we have heard or read. But I don't think Genesis 18:16-33 should lead us to some hyper-activism. I think our first 'doing' should be directed toward simply thinking, because we seldom think about the matters this text raises, namely: (1) how God stoops down to lure you to pray; (2) how God's righteous character forms the blessed bedrock of all your dealings with him; and (3) what a shield you might be in sheltering the people of this age from a judgment of God.

11

WHAT SODOM DOES TO YOU
(Genesis 19)

During one of our pastorates in Maryland, we lived in a town house for a year. My study was in the basement, which, as basements go, was fairly spacious and dry. However, the only natural light came in through small windows high up on the walls, and in the winter I heated the space with a portable kerosene heater which seemed to sport a bit of fumes. The absence of light tended to depress me and the presence of fumes gave headaches. Your surroundings can affect you in ways you may not have imagined. It was that way with Lot in Sodom; hence the title of this exposition—though we need to add the words 'and more' to it, for there is much more in this text than just how Sodom affected Lot. Perhaps we could come at Genesis 19 by thinking of the discoveries we make as we visit Sodom.

First, **we discover why the Bible worries over covenant drifting.** The Bible does worry, you know. There are hints of this anxiety already in chapter 13, where the text refers to the time before Yahweh destroyed Sodom and Gomorrah (v. 10), where it notes that Lot moved his tent 'as far as Sodom' (v. 12), and where it notes that the men of Sodom were evil and excessive sinners against Yahweh (v. 13). The Bible seems to be trembling over what is to come.

And you do see some changes come chapter 19. Lot is no longer in a tent but in 'the gate' (v. 1), in the hub of city government, and in a house (v. 2), a more permanent living situation. Lot has become 'urban.' Even when warned of the coming destruction, Lot 'lingered' (v. 16), so, as Kidner says, not even brimstone will make a pilgrim out of him. There is simply a certain sluggishness about him. In verses 17-22 one meets the term 'escape' five times, but somehow Lot is not very urgent about it. His wife looked back (v. 26), showing where her affections had settled. Afterwards Lot dwelt in a cave (v. 30) and his daughters demonstrated that they had sucked up some of the morality of Sodom (vv. 31-38). As one looks back over the narrative one can tally Lot's losses: he lost his moral discernment and backbone (vv. 7-8, offering his daughters to the mob); he lost the cogency of his witness (vv. 12-14, his prospective [?] sons-in-law thought he was joking); he lost a healthy sense of fear (vv. 16ff., his lingering); and he lost his family for God (vv. 26, 31-38). The only assurance we have about Lot himself is in 2 Peter 2:7-8.

So here is the danger of drifting. The angst of the Bible in Genesis 13:12 (Lot pitched his tent 'as far as Sodom') is justified. How do you suppose Lot justified the choice of Sodom? Perhaps life in the fast lane appealed to him; it may have been a good career move. There was likely more culture in Sodom than in Canaan's hills. Certainly more security—it was a well-watered area, perfect for Lot's livestock operation; there would be no more hand-to-mouth worry about finding adequate pasture. Sodom seemed to solve so many problems. He apparently had a position of some influence in the community, something his presence in the city gate (v. 1) suggests. And there were likely social advantages for the family—one might imagine equivalents of ballet, drama, and

YWCA softball. But his wife left her heart in Sodom, Sodom left its morality in his daughters, and, all in all, covenant drifting brought covenant disaster. I suppose there's nothing sinful in itself about a Sodom address, but it is stupid, and what is stupid can sometimes become tragic.

About the year 2000 there was a story in our Jackson, Mississippi newspaper, complete with pictures. It told of two men who had stolen a car, were being pursued by police officers, and, during the chase, tried to make a turn onto another street, and smashed into a concrete light pole. Pictures showed at least one of the men handcuffed and being tended to by medics. What was interesting, however, was that the suspects were using a pair of pliers to control the car because the steering wheel was missing. I suppose, when push comes to shove, one can use a pair of pliers to control a car, but it's not smart—not when you are in a hurry to get away from the local police! (Someone has told me that if a 'club' has been installed on a steering wheel to prevent theft that car thieves will then remove the whole steering apparatus in order to steal the car. However, one would think that thieves with a modicum of sense would make a point to steal a car that would not require such radical 'surgery'.) By the same token, I suppose it's possible for a man like Lot to live in Sodom—but it's not very smart.

Sometimes, as in Lot's case, it may take six chapters (13-19) before it all becomes obvious, before we discover that for Lot and Co. the 'cushiness' of life seems to matter more than the kingdom of God and that the city of man holds more attraction than the promise of God. We may not be too aware of it, but the drift occurs.

Someone like Demas may prove a New Testament analogue to Lot. Paul mentions Demas in the same breath as Luke, as sending greetings to the Colossian believers (Col. 4:14). But in 2 Timothy 4:10 Paul reports that Demas has deserted him, 'having loved the present age.' Quite a 'drift.' And of course there's a question that seems to come up for folks as they hear of such ones, like Demas. Folks ask, 'But was he *really* saved?' A. W. Tozer had the best answer to that, I think. He simply said that the last time we see Demas, he was walking in the wrong direction. And that can be true of you. You can be a member of First Presbyterian Church and be living in Sodom. And all we may be able to say is, 'The last time we saw her, she was walking in the wrong direction.'

Secondly, **we discover that the Bible shudders over divine judgment**. And we can begin by looking at the way the offense is described:

> ⁴Before they lay down, the men of the city, the men of Sodom, surrounded the house, from young to old, all the people, the whole lot of them. ⁵And they called to Lot and said to him, 'Where are the men who came to you tonight? Bring them out to us that we may know them.'

Verse 4 falls all over itself trying to underscore that the whole male population of Sodom was caught up in this plot and demand. Their wanting to 'know' (v. 5) these men clearly involves sexual 'knowledge'—the term is often used that way in Scripture. When Lot seeks to waylay their designs they threaten to work him over instead ('we'll deal worse with you than with them,' v. 9). It seems obvious that any number of Sodom's men were 'bisexual' and had wives, else Sodom would have had hardly any population. But all of them were seeking homosexual relations here—apparently they especially enjoyed homosexual gang rape of visitors. 'We'll show them a good ol' Sodom welcome!' was their attitude.

It seems quite clear that this was an aggravated, and not an isolated, offense. This is implicit in the pressure Lot put on his visitors. When they stated their intent to spend the night in the square (v. 2b), 'he put extreme pressure on them' (v. 3) and so they went to his house. Why did Lot press them so? Was he not driven by fear for them? Did he not likely know the risk they would be running? And why was he so eager for them to be on their way (v. 2)? Why the rush? Why not a tour of the city and the sights the next day? Why does Lot seem to suggest an early breakfast and perhaps a getaway before daylight? Why not hang around a bit? Because Lot knew what happened to visitors; he knew what was 'the usual'; he knew that visitors were repeatedly humiliated, made the object of 'fun' by the Sodom men. It was a practice that was utterly cruel—humiliating, harsh, horrid, and heartless. It was injustice and perversion in the highest.

There are those, of course, who object to this view of Genesis 19. Ours is a day when even biblical scholars like to engage in 're-interpretations.' So there are those who claim that when the men of Sodom wanted to 'know' the men, they were speaking of the 'know' of hospitality. Lot had squirrelled these visitors away to his house and they had not had the opportunity to meet them at all. But if nothing more, Lot's response in verse 8 implies what kind of 'knowing' is being considered— he there refers to his two daughters who had not 'known' a man. We're not talking about handshakes and introductions and smiles all round here. No, Sodom's men are intent on another evening of homosexual gang rape. Such a practice is linked in Israel's later covenant law with other forbidden sexual practices. According to Leviticus 18, Israel was to be different, not goose-stepping to the casual sexual customs of their near eastern neighbors (like Egypt and Canaan), and so 'Verboten' was written across a raft of perversions—incest in all its forms, adultery, homosexual practice, and bestiality.

And so the retribution comes. You know it's coming as you sense the sheer fear behind the angels' efforts to get Lot and his family to quit dawdling (vv. 12-22), as they try to teach Lot how to spell 'emergency.' The story reports the climactic and catastrophic moment in a mere two verses:

> And **Yahweh** rained down upon Sodom and upon Gomorrah burning sulfur—from Yahweh out of heaven. So he overthrew these cities as well as the whole plain and all the residents of the cities and the vegetation in the ground (vv. 24-25).

Verse 24 is quite an emphatic statement. The first 'Yahweh' is emphatic in the Hebrew text and the last clause repeats the same point: Yahweh rained down sulfur from Yahweh out of heaven. No need to consider 'secondary' causes that God might have used. Even the vegetation was blasted away (v. 25b). 'It is a fearful thing to fall into the hands of the living God' (Heb. 10:31). The Bible shudders over divine judgment.

Now all this leaves us asking a question and needing to get some perspective. Is there then no hope for those practicing such sexual perversions? The answer is no and yes. Paul does not mince words or pull punches in 1 Corinthians 6:9-10:

> Do you not know that the wicked will not inherit the kingdom of God? Do not be deceived: Neither the sexually immoral nor idolaters nor adulterers nor male prostitutes nor homosexual offenders nor thieves nor the greedy nor drunkards nor slanderers nor swindlers will inherit the kingdom of God (NIV).

That's quite clear. And we must remember that the emphasis here is on 'practicing' these offenses, as Galatians 5:21 stresses—Paul is not speaking of 'feelings' or 'tendencies' here, but actual and ongoing practice. The Greek terms Paul uses (which the NIV translates 'male prostitutes' and 'homosexual offenders') refer to both the so-called 'passive' and 'active' partners in such abuse. But this is not all that Paul says in this context, for verse 11 carries us beyond this seeming dead-end: 'And that is what some of you were. But you were washed, you were sanctified, you were justified in the name of the Lord Jesus Christ and by the Spirit of our God' (NIV). Now there is hope! In one of our former congregations I occasionally liked to use 1 Corinthians 6:9-11 as the 'call to worship' right at the beginning of a Sunday morning worship service. I could take them right through all the immorality and greed and booze and lies and nail them with 'And that's what some of you were!' And then continue: 'But you got yourselves washed' and so on. And then without a breather, tell them to stand and sing number 498, 'Jesus! What a Friend for Sinners!' Well, you may wonder about the disasters Paul mentions in verses 9-10—but where is Jesus going to get his church except from the wrecks in Satan's landfill? There is washing for your defilement; there is purifying for your pollution; there is acquittal for your guilt.

But you must not lose sight of the terrifying judgment of God. Jesus won't allow it. In fact, he had his own word for those who may have been too smug about Sodom:

> And you, Capernaum, will you be exalted to heaven? You will be brought down to Hades. For if the mighty works done in you had been done in Sodom, it would have remained until this day. But I tell you that it will be more tolerable on the day of judgment for the land of Sodom than for you (Matt. 11:23-24 RSV).

Sodom, Jesus says, still faces the last judgment, but there is something worse than Sodom's premier offense related in Genesis 19; the 'something worse' is being engulfed with the privileges of the presence and power of Jesus, as Capernaum had been, and being unmoved by it all. And we are in Capernaum's sandals. Here in this congregation just within the last week or so, we have heard the testimony to Jesus' resurrection on Easter Sunday, and—if you were listening— you heard arguments given for why that testimony is reliable and not a pipe-dream. And over the months and years you have heard the gospel story, and, again, with adequate reasons for why that account is reliable—the apostles preached that story to audiences that included Jesus' and their enemies and they had to be precise with their facts and assertions or they would've been blown off the historical map as just another bunch of deceivers. You can have all that, can have the resurrection gospel, evidences of its reliability; you can have all these advantages and yet you've never confessed Jesus as Messiah or submitted to him as Lord. If Sodom had had your advantages it would have repented. Jesus said so.

Imagine if some of the fellows from Sodom could come into this church service tonight. Oh, you'd probably pull your kids a little closer to you. Can you imagine one of them stopping at your pew and pulling out a hymnbook, leafing through it, finding the Westminster Confession of Faith and the Shorter Catechism in the back of it. He might say, 'My, we didn't have this.' He might pull out one of those ESV pew Bibles, flip through it, turn to you and ask, 'You have this in your own language, no less?' True, they did not repent of their twisted sexual perversions and heartlessness. But what of you? You have what they never had. You have the full data on Jesus and yet you refuse to lay hold of him! It will be more tolerable on the day of judgment for the land of Sodom than for you. How the Bible shudders over—and under—divine judgment.

Finally, we discover that **how the Bible prizes intercessory prayer** (vv. 27-29). Abraham's heart must have bounced off the pit of his stomach that morning as he looked toward Sodom and Gomorrah and saw the plumes of smoke (vv. 27-28). There's a certain pathos that breathes out of verses 27-28 in view of 18:22-33 and Abraham's dogged pleading with Yahweh—all the way down to the tally of ten righteous. But appearances were misleading, for actually 'God remembered Abraham' (v. 29), and though he did not answer the *form* of Abraham's prayer, he answered the *substance* of it, even if he had to drag Lot out of Sodom to do it. So these three verses could not be left out of the story—the writer simply had to tell what happened to Abraham's prayer! God did not fulfill the precise conditions of his petition, but he did fulfill the clear intent of it. Sometimes that is the way God operates with our prayers.

B. M. Palmer, in his book of prayer, tells of a case personally known to him—a woman who had been away for a whole summer from her family (apparently they were in Britain or Europe). She was so eager to return to them and was overwhelmed with anguish when she discovered that all the rooms in a certain steamer were already engaged and that she would have to wait two more weeks in New York before she could get passage home. This was cause for bitter tears. But her tears ceased and she was sobered when within a few days she received word that the vessel on which she craved passage was buried at the bottom of the ocean. As Dr Palmer said, the prayer was denied, only that it might be answered. The intent of her prayer was answered, the precise conditions were not.

Sometimes you will find that is the way the Lord deals with you and—in any case, he never despises but always prizes intercessory prayer.

So…here in Genesis 19 we have covenant drifting, divine judgment, and intercessory prayer. Strange, isn't it, how the Bible never deals in trivialities?

12

WHEN FAITH DOESN'T SHOW UP
(Genesis 20)

When our eldest son was a one-year-old he was fascinated with the toilet stool in the bathroom, probably because it was one thing that was down at his level and because he loved reaching his hands down in the 'bowl' and splashing the water. I wouldn't say that we, as parents, were severely 'moralistic', but we gave him to know, by whacks that could be felt through his diaper, that such toilet play was wrong in our view. One evening I saw him exiting the bathroom, shaking his head from side to side, and saying authoritatively, 'No, No, No!' He knew it was on the list of prohibited behaviors—but he had just done it again (even if deeply convicted about it). It is utter folly to assume that once a child realizes something is wrong, he will never do it again.

We face something similar in Genesis 20. Something like what Genesis 20 tells us about happened before in 12:10-20 (indeed, we find Isaac pulling the same move in Genesis 26). Some biblical critics assume that if a miscue like this occurred in chapter 12, it surely couldn't or wouldn't happen again. They would say that these three accounts must be variations of only one episode.

But I doubt it. J. C. Ryle (in *Light from Old Times*) wrote a paper on the puritan Samuel Ward. But he said he had a great deal of difficulty doing so, because no less than three divines named 'S. Ward' lived in the first half of the seventeenth century—and they were all members of Sydney College, Cambridge. Two were Samuel Wards and one was Seth Ward. Ryle had to try to untangle the skein of their respective biographical details. There wasn't really only one; there were actually three. So with similar biblical events—we need to be careful about trying to steam-iron them into one. After the near disaster of Genesis 12:10-20 we may think the same sort of thing wouldn't happen again, but here in chapter 20 we have a different time and circumstances, if the same kind of failure. Here in verse 13 Abraham admits his behavior was a set *policy* he followed, so repeats are perfectly expectable.

So here in Genesis 20 we are in Gerar, which may be about fifteen miles northwest of Beersheba. But what possibly can we learn from this dismal episode where faith doesn't show up?

First, we learn of **the recurring inconsistency of God's servants** (vv. 1-2, 11-13). It *is* a bit surprising to us readers after 12:10-12. Surely we will not meet that failure again. But here it is: 'And Abraham said about Sarah his wife, "She is my sister." So Abimelech, king of Gerar, sent and took Sarah' (v. 2). Later, when Abimelech confronted him, Abraham tries to 'explain' what drove him to it. There was his fear ('I said, "Surely, there is no fear of God in this place—and they shall kill me because of my wife,"' v. 11). And then there was, believe it or not, several grains of truth in what he said, for Sarah really was his half-sister (v. 12). But, perhaps primarily, there was a long-standing policy he had always followed—wherever they wandered, Sarah would always pass Abraham off as her brother (v. 13). With no little kids running around the tent, it could seem convincing. Of course, as in chapter 12, never mind the danger Abraham was putting Sarah in, the risks they ran by this expedient. So…you come from seeing Abraham as a paragon of intercession in chapter 18 to seeing him as a practitioner of deception in chapter 20.

Again, we must note what this is—it is a failure of faith. Abraham had the assurance of 12:3 ('I will bless your blessers, and the one who despises you I will curse') but didn't rub it into the picky details of life in Gerar. It's not that the Lord had not made a covenant with him, not that the Lord had not been gracious toward him, not that he could not remember God's promises—but it all didn't trickle down into a scary situation in Gerar.

Now if you are a Christian that is likely true of you. Most of your failures do not come because you suddenly doubt the doctrines of the Trinity or of Jesus' resurrection, nor because you have ceased believing in Jesus' second coming or his atoning death. It's not that I, for example, don't believe in the sovereignty of God—of course I do, until I rush out for an appointment and see I have a flat tyre/tire on my pick-up. I do fine in my faith until I hear I have a tumor in my colon, or see an Abimelech looking at my wife with a gleam in his eye. I trust the Lord for my eternal salvation, but just not in this perplexity on Thursday morning. Doctrinal faith does not become daily faith.

I have always been amused by the anecdote Paul Johnson tells about Bertrand Russell (in *Intellectuals*). Russell the mathematician, philosopher, and pacifist (apparently sometimes a pugnacious pacifist) loved tea but, even if his life depended on it, could not make tea. His wife once left him step-by-step, line-upon-line instructions on how to make tea—and he failed miserably. There's something wrong with someone who can't handle the mundane level of things! It makes one begin to think: if a fellow can't make tea, there must be something wrong with pacifism too! So our faith must be able to operate actively in the dust and dirt of the daily.

But let's go back to our main point—the 'recurring inconsistency' of God's servants. We recall that 'Abraham's folly' had happened before—almost disastrously (12:10-20). So don't be so amazed at yourself. Don't be shocked if once more you find yourself controlled by your fears rather than resting in promises. Don't be surprised if you find yourself living by un-faith again. Don't say stupid things like: 'God will never have to teach me that lesson again.' O yes, he will. Don't forget Romans 7:18-19.

Secondly, we learn here of **the surprising evaluation of human sin** (vv. 3-6). Abimelech takes Sarah into his harem. Some expositors point out that nothing is mentioned here about Sarah's beauty. Perhaps age had taken some of its toll and Abimelech's concern was more on cementing a political/military agreement with her 'brother.' Abimelech had had no sexual relations with Sarah yet, but her time would no doubt come. Then God speaks to Abimelech in a dream and tells him he's—as we sometimes say—'dead meat.' Let's simply pick up the story via verses 3-6:

> [3]Then God came to Abimelech in a dream at night, and he said, 'Look, you're a dead man because of the woman you've taken—she's a married woman.' [4]But Abimelech had not gone near her, and he said, 'Lord, will you kill even a righteous nation? [5]Did not he himself say to me, "She is my sister," and she—even she—said, "He is my brother." In the honesty of my heart and in the innocence of my hands I have done this.' [6]And God said to him in the dream, 'Yes, I know that it was in the honesty of your heart you did this, and it was I who held you back from sinning against me. Therefore I did not allow you to touch her....'

Did you catch the viewpoint of verse 6? 'Sinning against me.' The surprising evaluation of human sin! Welcome to the strange world within the Bible, the book that evaluates things in ways that we can't fathom. It's something like the time a journalist asked Pope John XXIII how many people work in the Vatican. The pope pondered the matter, as if he were mentally calculating what the total tally might be, then, deadpan, he replied, 'About half' (Marty Grothe, *Viva la Repartee*). It was a completely different angle on the matter.

That's what we have here. God so much as told Abimelech that it was his providence that kept him from sleeping with Sarah and thereby 'sinning against me,' rather than sinning against her husband. But in the Ancient Near East it was different. Nahum Sarna (*Exodus*, 114) tells us that there adultery was a private wrong committed against the husband—it was an infringement of his exclusive rights of possession. And though in Egypt and Ugarit adultery was dubbed the 'great sin,' the gods had no role in restraining it nor in seeing that legal consequences ensued. But in Israel adultery not only hurt people but also defied God. In Israel, adultery was an offense against God. That assumption persists through the Scriptures: 'Let marriage be held in honor among all, and let the marriage bed be undefiled; for God will judge the immoral and adulterous' (Heb. 13:4 esv). You may say, 'But this is a conservative Presbyterian church!' And you may say that I am surely 'preaching to the choir' here—but choirs need to be preached to. Don't imagine this has nothing to do with congregations of God's people.

In John Gresham's novel *The Testament* there's a conversation between Father Phil, rector of an Episcopal flock in Maryland, and Nate O'Reilly. They are sawing up two-by-fours in the process of remodeling children's classrooms in the church building. They take a break and are sitting on the floor, sipping their latte. Father Phil grins and informs Nate that he missed a great sermon yesterday. Nate asks where it was preached, Phil retorted, 'Here, of course.' What was the subject, Nate wanted to know. Adultery. Nate asks, 'For it or against it?' Phil was solid: 'Against it, as always.' Nate opines that he doesn't think adultery would be much of a problem with Phil's congregation. But Phil assures Nate that he gives the sermon once a year. The same sermon, but always fresh. You get the point? One doesn't say, 'Oh, but they're all card-carrying Episcopalians!' No, one preaches the same sermon to them once a year…because that's where it's needed.

We must watch our attitudes then. Don't say, 'O I'm a Christian man,' or, 'I'm a Christian woman, and I would never…' You don't know what you'd do given a certain set of circumstances. Rather your prayer ought always to be that God would do for you what he did for Abimelech—hold you back from sinning against him (v. 6).

Once more, we learn of **the gracious benefits from God's agent** (vv. 7, 17-18). So God orders Abimelech to restore Abraham's wife to him, and then tells him that Abraham is his agent—'He is a prophet, and he will pray for you and you will live' (v. 7a). He identifies Abraham as a 'prophet' and underscores his function as an intercessor.

Abimelech's problem was that 'Yahweh had completely closed every womb in Abimelech's household because of Sarah, Abraham's wife' (v. 18). Perhaps it took a little time for Abimelech to realize this, but when no one was getting pregnant it must have become apparent that something was wrong. Then it was when Abraham prayed for him that 'God healed Abimelech and his wife and his slave girls, so that they could give birth' (v. 17).

I suppose we readers become uneasy and cringe over the fact that finky Abraham is cast in the role of 'prophet' here, that the one who deceives Abimelech is the one through whom Abimelech is restored. It simply seems so out of sync. But Abraham is a prophet by God's appointment, not by human merit. God appointed Abraham to function as a channel by which he would bless the nations (12:3b), and so Abraham was to function as such a channel of blessing to others even in his own lifetime. He had been more of a scourge to Abimelech than anything, but now at God's direction, he becomes a conveyor of blessing. Hence we see the gracious benefits from God's agent.

There is a sense in which none of us shares Abraham's unique position as the channel of blessing to the nations, but all the same God does sometimes place us in an *Abraham-like position*. I am thinking in individual terms, especially of Christian parents and of fathers in particular. If you are a Christian father, are you not to be a 'prophet' in your own household? Are you not charged to bring the word of God to them? But are you not also to be a prophet in the sense that Abraham was here in Genesis 20? You are to be an intercessor for them. If you don't pray for your spouse and children, who will? Well, maybe a good many folks! But shouldn't they be your special charge? And your prayers are not for them to go to some elite university or to get a lucrative job, but rather that they will have a soft heart toward the gospel of Jesus and that they will want to be slaves of Christ however it is that they may earn a living. You are meant to be God's agent of blessing in your own household. *Your greatest work will be done on your knees before you ever leave for work in the morning.*

Fourthly, we learn here of **the solid comfort of God's vigilance** (vv. 3-7). There was such folly here. Abraham once more exposed Sarah to danger. God had promised them a son via Sarah, even in their old age (18:1-15), but here was Abraham letting Sarah fend for herself and become the object of Abimelech's nocturnal attentions whenever he might get around to it. So here you see the faithfulness of God in living color: he is faithful to his promise ('I am your shield,' 15:1) even when his servant doesn't live by that promise. He simply intervenes here. 'You will surely die,' he tells Abimelech. It's as if he said to the king, Yes, yes, I know you didn't realize she was his wife, but she is, and you must restore her to her husband or you and yours will be terminated, no bones about it (cf. v. 7). How mighty and vigilant God's protection is here! The fault was Abraham's—

he was walking by fear rather than by faith, but God refused to allow his 'church'—consisting of Abraham and Sarah—to be swallowed up (see Psalm 105:12-15). So this episode gives us reason to believe the doctrine of *the indestructibility of the church*. Does this mean that every individual who shares Abraham's faith will be kept from danger or death? No, but it means that God will never allow his covenant people to be eradicated in this world.

Naturally, we may wonder about that, for most of the time in these days it seems like the lives of Abraham's faith-family are cheap and disposable. There were 138 snuffed out in northern Nigeria, locked in a church by Boko Haram terrorists, who detonated bombs; then, if any tried to escape, they were either gunned down or their throats were cut. Or there's North Korea, where executions are carried out in a stadium as a public spectacle. Or there's a Syrian Christian family living in Alexandria, Egypt (likely refugees from their homeland), and they are stabbed to death in their own home. The church seems so fragile and Satan's thugs wipe them out seemingly at will. But then one reads of a baptismal service for 228 Iranian believers. They went across the border into another country, so they could hold the service without danger of interruption. But those confessors of Christ would go back to their own land, and they knew what might very well await them. But there is the church of Jesus—growing in Iran, of all places. God keeps showing us that his eye remains on his fragile people and that Jesus is preserving his oft-battered sheep. 'Yahweh will never forsake his people, and he will never abandon his heritage' (Ps. 94:14).

There will be times when faith doesn't show up. But Genesis 20 tells us more; it says that there will be times when faith doesn't show up—but God does!

13

Laughter and anguish in the Covenant
(Genesis 21)

There's a story about Calvin Coolidge when he was Vice President. He was enduring a dinner party, and the lady sitting next to him commented on how silent he was and yet insisted that he really must talk to her. She divulged that she had made a bet that day that she could get more than two words out of him. Coolidge turned to her and said, 'You lose.' Now some biblical narratives are like Mr Coolidge—they are very terse and reserved, especially in reference to God and what he is doing. One thinks of passages like Genesis 37 or Exodus 2:1-10 or 1 Samuel 27, where God is not even mentioned in the text at all. Those texts are a special challenge in that one must try to figure out how God is involved in the events they narrate. But other passages have profuse references to God and to his activity. Like Genesis 21. And yet, like Hagar (v. 19), we need our eyes opened to see him here. So once more we come with our question—How is the covenant God operating here, how is he working?

So, first, in Genesis 21 we need to note **the promise God keeps** (vv. 1-7). In these verses we find relief, obedience, and wonder. We find our relief in verses 1-2:

> ¹Now Yahweh looked out for Sarah as he had said, and Yahweh did for Sarah as he had promised. ²So Sarah became pregnant and gave birth to a son for Abraham in his old age, at the appointed time which God had promised him.

If we've really been caught up in the 'Abraham story' we have been longing for something like this since 11:30 (Sarai barren—had no child). To some degree we enter into the ups and downs of Abraham and Sarah's faith, longing for the 'seed' to come. And now at last we get our literary antacid, relieving the tension of the narrative to this point. Three statements in these two verses (vv. 1a, 1b, 2b) underscore Yahweh's faithfulness to his word.

And then we meet obedience and wonder as well. Obedience in naming the child (v. 3, see 17:19) and in circumcising him (v. 4, see 17:10-12). And wonder overflows in verses 5-7, especially over Abraham's age (v. 5) and God's 'joke' on Sarah's behalf (vv. 6-7). This was simply not 'supposed' to happen (18:11)—no gynecologist gave Sarah a prayer. I suppose it was something like the day Chris Hoyle was sitting at her desk in an office building in Walnut Creek, California. She heard someone screaming and looked up to see a man falling past her window, head down, feet up. She hustled down to ground level of the five-stories, went outside, and shouted at a man standing near the building, asking if everyone was all right because she had just seen a man fall off the roof. 'Yeah, that would be me,' Ken Larsen told her. He had been laying telecommunications cable up on the roof, along with his co-worker, and he had taken one too many steps backwards. His arm was scratched, his shoulder bruised, but nothing broken—and he had landed on his feet! One doesn't wish ill to Mr Larsen, but there's a sense in which such things ought not to happen. One shouldn't be able to fall five stories and come out of it unharmed.

But, of course, we're dealing with a far greater 'impossibility' than that here. In case you missed it, in verses 1-7 we are not dealing with anything common here—it is *Yahweh's* doing; it is supernatural. The first occurrence of 'Yahweh' in verse 1 is emphatic in the Hebrew text, as if to stress this point. The impossible promise has come to pass.

And yet doesn't God's work here pack a further assurance for God's people? Think it through. If God *begins* his people in this world by such an impossible act, it means there is something 'supernatural' about them, and therefore it means that nothing and no one will ever be able to overcome or overthrow or annihilate this people. They are a miracle people. Their impossible beginning carries with it their certain preservation.

When I was a lad, my neighborhood friend and I would often play 'cowboys' with our six-shooter cap guns that we wore in holsters on our 'gun-belts.' We didn't know it was politically incorrect—and it wouldn't have mattered to us anyway. But it was frustrating for me, for if, while sneaking around next-door neighbor, Mr Brown's, garage, I happened to get the drop on Tom, I would holler 'Bam! Bam!' as I 'shot' him. But he refused to die. He would say, 'You can't shoot me—I'm tight bones.' Now what did that mean? Was tight bones a comic book character who was impervious to injury? Or was it a philosophical concept of some sort? I never found out. But the context makes enough clear—whatever 'tight bones' precisely was, it meant that Tom's body was so condensed, so compacted, and concentrated and compressed that no missile, even an imaginary one, could penetrate it. He was indestructible.

That's the way the covenant people are. Jesus tells us he has a 'tight bones' people: 'Now this is the will of the One who sent me, that I should lose nothing of all that he has given me but raise it up at the last day' (John 6:39). Will his people be lost, for example, by the ravages of death? No way—Jesus will raise them up at the last day. His are a people that are infallibly secure and kept through whatever all comers throw at them. 'He will sustain you to the end' (1 Cor. 1:8). That's the implication we derive here from the promise that God keeps.

How quickly the story's mood changes! Now in verses 8-13 we see **the pain God authorizes**. The occasion is several years down the time-line. Abraham threw a party because Isaac had been weaned. This occurred much later than among most of us. It was not unusual for a child to be three years old or more before being weaned. So Ishmael would have been sixteen or seventeen years old at this point (cf. 17:25).

It is not exactly clear what Ishmael's offense was. Actually, his name is not used in verse 9—he is simply called 'the son of Hagar.' The verb root that describes what Ishmael is doing is the root from which we get the name 'Isaac' (laughter). The word can sometimes mean 'joking' (Gen. 19:14) or to 'mock' (cf. Gen. 39:14, 17) or to 'entertain' (as the Philistines want blind Samson to do in Judges 16:25, meaning something like 'provide us an occasion to mock him'). Ishmael's laughing at the toddler seems to have been a derisive laughter, laden with mockery and ridicule. It was his way of despising or disdaining Abraham and his seed (see 12:3) and perhaps an initial fulfillment of 16:12.

Sarah has no doubts about what must be done—both the slave-wife and her son must be driven out (v. 10); Ishmael must not share the inheritance with Sarah's son, Isaac. This puts Abraham in a bind, both affectionately and legally. Abraham doubtless cherished a real affection for Ishmael, but then he seems also to have recognized Ishmael as his legitimate son and heir (cf. 16:2; 17:18). Nahum Sarna points to a possible 'loophole.' There is a clause in the laws of Lipit-Ishtar (*c.* 1870 B.C.) in which a father may grant freedom to the slave-woman and the children she has borne him, and in that case they forfeit their share in the paternal property. Sarna suggests that Sarah is demanding that Abraham exercise that option. It seems severe and harsh—and Sarah probably wanted it to be so. In any case, Abraham is loath to do this (v. 11). (Time was when Abraham had followed Sarah's advice [Gen. 16], and it had led to this whole Hagar-Ishmael fiasco.)

However, God overruled Abraham's reluctance and specifically directed him to assent to Sarah's demand: 'As far as all that Sarah says to you—listen to her voice, for it is in Isaac that your seed will be designated' (v. 12b). The chosen line will run through Isaac. And yet one can almost 'hear' how painful this was for Abraham in (the rather difficult) verse 14, as it dwells on each individual detail: 'So Abraham rose early in the morning and took bread and a skin of water and gave (them) to Hagar; he placed (them) on her shoulder; and (he gave her) the child as well, and sent her off. So she went and wandered around in the wilderness of Beer-sheba.'

There may be some 'overspill' from this text for us. These nasty circumstances here in chapter 21 are the fruit of what Abraham and Sarah began in chapter 16 with their let's-help-God-out procedure. And now here God is directing them in this painful way, pain which actually arises from Abraham and Sarah's own errors. That may be a point we ought to observe: sometimes when God leads us through or out of the circumstances we have wrongfully arranged, there is no painless, ouch-less way out.

Perhaps only males will understand this analogy. Let's say a fellow is working in his shop or garage, and one of his tools goes awry and nicks or gouges his leg. It's not serious, but he applies some antibiotic ointment and slaps a Band-Aid on it.

In a day or so, he decides he can take the Band-Aid off. Then he faces a dilemma, or at least a decision. Being a guy, he likely has a hairy leg. So he can either take the bandage off very slowly and feel the twinge of every hair involved being pulled; or he can mentally psych himself and rip it off suddenly, so that all the pain is concentrated in one moment. But either way, it's going to hurt. We sometimes need such a reminder. Some of us have such a 'we can fix this' attitude that it's hard to realize that we can't. Some consequences are not reversible, some messes are not totally cleanable. In Abraham-mode, we are called to walk on from the broken pieces, from the circumstances that can't be rectified, and seek to be faithful from that point.

Thirdly, we should note **the pity God shows** (vv. 14-21). As noted, Hagar's situation was grievously sad (v. 14), and soon became seemingly hopeless (vv. 15-16). With the water gone and apparently both exhausted, Hagar deposits the lad near a shrub and takes herself a ways off, as if distance will alleviate the unbearable sight of the lad's demise. Of course, she did have the promise of 16:10-12, but we are not prone to remember promises or think through their implications when we are in the thick of distress. But God intervenes. Twice in verse 17 we hear (by the writer and then the angel of God) that 'God heard' the lad's voice, the verb likely being a play on the name Ishmael ('God hears,' although, strangely enough the lad is never called *by name* in 21:1-21). God heard the lad's voice, not Hagar's. And God reaffirms his promise: 'I will make him into a great nation' (v. 18b).

Verse 19 then tells of God's provision: 'Then God opened her eyes and she saw a well of water! She went and filled the water skin and gave the lad a drink.' The well was likely there all the time, but Hagar, in her distress and turmoil, apparently didn't see it. After this crisis point is past, we read the terse wrap-up of the segment:

²⁰Now God was with the lad and he grew; and he lived in the wilderness and became an archer. ²¹And he lived in the wilderness of Paran, and his mother took for him a wife from the land of Egypt.

There is not only God's critical provision (v. 19) but also his ongoing care: 'God was with the lad' (v. 20a). The pity of heaven met the immediate crisis and went on upholding over the long haul.

What do we make of Hagar and Ishmael here? Here is Ishmael, who was mocking and disdaining the covenant heir, and he is sent away. And yet for all that, he is still cared for by God. We might say that verses 15-19 give us a basis for what is sometimes called 'common grace': just because folks are not part of the covenant people does not mean that God does not do them good. On the contrary, their lives are held in his hands and he sustains them.

Jesus has told us that our Father 'makes his sun rise on the evil and the good and causes it to rain upon the righteous and the unrighteous' (Matt. 5:45; see Acts 14:17).

God's pity in such cases means that we have no reason to write such people off our compassion. Perhaps you can think of a relative or friend. You have been able to set the gospel before this person, to tell them freely of Christ, what he has done for you and means to you—but he wants no truck with it. Perhaps he was nasty in his refusal or maybe he wasn't. He may have simply told you 'Thanks, but no thanks.' But the gospel got the stiff arm. What then do you do? Simply write such folks off? Do you tell your kids that the family isn't going to Uncle Ernie's place for a family get-together, because he just doesn't have any interest in the gospel and it's a waste of time to hang out with him and Aunt Madge? They are not conversion fodder that we then can put on the side-rails of life. Or…do you go on treating those friends or relatives kindly and considerately and attentively, perhaps remembering that your kindness toward them for Jesus' sake may be all that they have. Oh, these folks may have spouse and children and education and success in career and enjoyable hobbies and a beach house…but no hope at all; so the least you can do is to maintain your interest and friendship with them and pity them as God pities them.

Lastly, we need to notice **the provision God gives** (vv. 22-34). Shades of Genesis 20! Abimelech is back! He comes with Phicol, his troop commander (v. 22), which suggests a military matter may be involved, apparently a mutual nonaggression pact of some sort (cf. v. 23). Abimelech appears to see something 'uncanny' about Abraham—'God is with you,' he confesses, 'in whatever you do.' There may be a bit of a contrast here: Abimelech is drawn to Abraham, while Ishmael repudiates the covenant heir.

Abimelech may also be eager for a definite commitment with Abraham in view of Abraham's 'shifty' dealing with Abimelech in chapter 20. That may have left Abimelech uneasy and he may have wanted to nail down an overt agreement with this powerful chieftain. In any case, Abraham is willing to swear a covenant oath with Abimelech (v. 24), but at the same time he complains to Abimelech about a water well Abimelech's servants had taken over from Abraham's men (v. 25). Abimelech may toot his own kindness (v. 23b) if he likes, but if his hired men act like a bunch of thugs it doesn't go down very well. Of course, Abimelech denies knowing anything about this matter until just now (v. 26). That may have been true, and, then again, he could have been 'blowing smoke,' as we say. For this reason Abraham stuck an extra clause, as it were, into the covenant arrangement—he gave Abimelech seven ewe lambs, which Abimelech accepted as testimony that Abraham had dug the well in question (or perhaps another well that Abraham's servants had since dug;

vv. 28-30). 'Therefore he called the name of that place Beer-sheba—it was when both of them swore an oath there' (v. 31).

But I want you especially to notice verses 33-34: 'And he planted a tamarisk tree in Beer-sheba. And he called there on the name of Yahweh, the everlasting God. Then Abraham sojourned in the land of the Philistines many days.' Yahweh is *el 'olam*, the everlasting God. The idea may refer to reaching as far back in the past as one can imagine and/or it may refer to the farthest reaches of the future, in which case Yahweh is the one who holds all that future and all his people's fortunes in it (cf. Psalm 90:1-2). Yahweh is the forever-God! But note the following verb in verse 34: 'Abraham sojourned,' a verb that connotes a passing, fragile, temporary, I-don't-really-belong kind of life. It's quite an ironic contrast: in his fleeting life he worships an everlasting God.

Doesn't that ever strike you here in this assembly? In our morning worship we usually sing the Gloria Patri right after we confess our faith in the creed. Doesn't it ever grab you as you sing, 'As it [the Trinity] was in the beginning, is now, and ever shall be—world without end'? Here you are, a passing piece of human clay, sojourning in South Carolina, holding on to the back of the pew in front of you and yet lifting praise to an everlasting God! Indeed, isn't that, isn't he, the only hope you have? Of course, all this was implied in the covenant promise of 17:7. If Yahweh once says, 'I will be God to you,' then there is no condition or circumstance when that can stop being true. He wraps your sojourning in his foreverness.

But we want to notice here not only the sojourner's worship but the Lord's gifts. And what did God grant to Abraham in this situation? Peace with Abimelech and certified rights to a well. You may not get too excited over wells (especially if you're on 'city water'), but wells are essential when you have gobs of livestock as Abraham did. I would think that this little gift (as we may view it) must have served as a big assurance to Abraham. It was only a well, to be sure, a bit of ordinary provision, but clearly a token that God was providing for him. That was the God Abraham worshiped: the forever God who looks out for every day needs, the God of eternity caring for his servant in time. Only a well...well, because that's what he needed at the time. God gave him peace and water. And that's not bad.

Sometimes we are in our Hagar-mode, and need our eyes opened (v. 19), to see all the ways God is actively at work in our case.

14

FAITH FACES THE PERPLEXITY OF GOD
(Genesis 22)

Once, while I was teaching at Reformed Seminary in Mississippi, I came across a note one of our sons had left lying somewhere. He was probably around ten at the time. In this note he was scalding in his bitterness and hatred for the seminary, mentioned how he disdained the current president (whom he mentioned by name). It went on for some lines, a sort of what-all-I-hate-about-my-life. I was buffaloed. And, of course, one turns psychological almost immediately—this hostility is really directed at me and he's projecting it on to other entities. One envisions counseling sessions in which a child 'advocate' reams one out for being such a cruel, insensitive, dense and uncaring father. Had I not spent enough time with him, after all? Why such a tirade? I showed it to my secretary, a wonderful mother figure, and she had no light to offer. He didn't seem to have a chip on his shoulder in coming days, no evidence of a grudge. So some days afterwards I asked Seth about it. He said, 'Oh, Thursday was "Opposite Day,"' a day when the school kids could put down the exact reverse of what they really thought. Well, that cleared that up, but, at the time, I was totally blind-sided.

So was Abraham. He couldn't see it coming when God said to him, 'Take now your son, your only one, whom you love—Isaac, and go off to the land of Moriah and offer him up there as a burnt-offering on one of the mountains which I will point out to you' (v. 2). We readers, of course, have the readers' edge, in that we are informed that God was testing Abraham (v. 1) in all this. And yet we are shocked by the suddenness of it all and by the focus of the test, Abraham's dear son (v. 2). Genesis 22 is a fascinating, full, and puzzling narrative and we must be careful that we don't get stuck in some false starts with it.

False starts? Like what? Like turning the focus of the test into an accusation of Abraham, saying that Abraham had begun to love God's gift (Isaac) more than God himself. That is always a danger, but the text does not say that was the case. And please don't become inebriated over drawing connections to Christ and riding off on your New Testament horse too quickly. It is not likely, for example, that Isaac is a 'type' of Christ, for Isaac himself had a ram sacrificed *for* him. So, if anything, Isaac represents Israel in his/their need. We need to stick with the Old Testament text until we understand it, before we go sailing off to establish links to the New Testament.

Furthermore, don't be put off by accusations that this account is pagan-like and sadistic. It may *seem* so, but it's this very alleged quality that supports the factuality of the event related. The last thing Israel would want to do would be to depict Yahweh in a non-attractive way, as if he were an ogre of some sort. The very fact that this brutal story 'made the cut' and stands in Israel's scriptures argues for its having-happenedness, for Israel had every reason to suppress it. Israel would hardly concoct a story like this. Yet here it stands—apparently simply because it's true. And, oddly enough, the upshot of the whole story shows that Yahweh wants no part of human sacrifice.

Faith, however, must face the perplexity of God. And what do you do in such circumstances? Our text says that *when God is not clear you go on walking in the darkness by faith and obedience until he brings the light.* So let's move on into the main segments of the text.

Look first at verses 1-2 and consider **the problem of God's ways**:

> [1]After these things God tested Abraham, and said to him, 'Abraham!' And he said, 'Yes?' [2]Then he said, 'Take now your son, your only one, whom you love—Isaac, and go off to the land of Moriah and offer him up there as a burnt-offering on one of the mountains which I will point out to you.'

As John Sailhamer points out (*Expositor's Bible Commentary*), this request or demand is surprising even for the reader, for nothing to this point has provided any clue that something like this might be in the offing. We are as surprised as Abraham. And the demand is clearly wrenching—that comes across in the phrase-by-anguished-phrase build-up of the language in verse 2: your son/your only one/whom you love/Isaac. The knife goes in deeper with every phrase. It may, by the way, have brought to mind another wrenching experience: the words 'go off' (lit., 'go off by/for yourself') in verse 2 are the very ones used also in 12:1, when Abraham was called to peel himself away from all that was familiar and cherished and go off to an undisclosed destination. Now in chapter 22, years later, there comes another 'forsaking' moment. But perhaps what strikes us most about God's demand is that it is so seemingly absurd. We have ridden through the drama of Abraham and Sarah's childlessness for almost a dozen chapters. Finally Yahweh came through on his promise (21:1) and assured Abraham that Isaac would be the conduit through whom the covenant people would flourish in this world (21:12). And now, in 22:2, God's command flies in the face of God's promise. The matter is gut-wrenching, but that is not the worst of it. The real problem is that *God is contradicting his own word*. At least it appears that way.

Let's make some allowances. We must admit that individual believers today are not exactly in the same position as Abraham. Abraham was the head of the covenant people and in that sense he holds a position that I, for example, do not share. But after one makes certain distinctions some hard facts remain. There are still Abraham-like situations that God's people tend to face and the text invites you to ponder this fact and dilemma. We don't face Abraham's particular trial, but we face his generic trial, times when God's ways seem to contradict the assurances of his own word. Don't you face times when God's ways do not seem to match up with his own declared character, when, given the mess he is taking you through, he doesn't seem to be your refuge and strength, a well-proved help in troubles (Ps. 46:1)? Nor is Jesus any different: he hears of Lazarus' dire illness and stays two days longer where he was (John 11:6). Hard to see how that squares with 'Now Jesus loved Martha and her sister and Lazarus' (11:5). When the Westminster Shorter Catechism asks, 'What is God?', the answer is: 'God is a Spirit, infinite, eternal, and unchangeable in his being, wisdom, power, holiness, justice, goodness, and truth, and perplexity.' No, that's not quite it; I added that last 'attribute.' But it just might as well be there. These first two verses want to flag this truth for us. God is not always clear, and it doesn't matter how much Reformed theology you've read or even if you personally know R. C. Sproul, there will be times when you cannot make head nor tail of what God is doing. There may be times when everything you thought you knew about

God is up for grabs, when God seems to be so strange that he doesn't seem to be himself. But the first of Genesis 22 at least helps cushion us for such times, for it tells us that very likely we are going to have problems with God's ways.

Secondly, in all this perplexity we must note **the pathway of God's servant** (vv. 3-8). That pathway consists of simple obedience: 'So Abraham rose early in the morning, saddled up his donkey...and went to the place God had designated to him' (v. 3). So disappointing! Well, all of verses 3-6 are disappointing—in that they simply report Abraham's obedience almost in matter-of-fact form. Our anguish-loving culture thrives on psychological striptease and all we get is bare obedience. Can you imagine how it would go if one of the cable news shows had gotten Abraham for a 'morning after' interview? The dashing blonde presenter would lean over, narrow her eyes, and ask, 'But Abraham, how did you *feel* when God demanded that you sacrifice Isaac?' Yes, let the emotions roll down like an ever-flowing stream! But the text simply stresses Abraham's quiet obedience. That doesn't mean there was no trauma or tension or even emotions; there is plenty to grip your guts in verses 2, 7-8, and in the slow-motion camera movement of verses 9-10. Yes, plenty of angst. But that does not figure in the immediate response in verses 3-6. Here is simply a report of obedience. What was Abraham's response? He simply began to do what God had told him to do.

But what is it that *sustains* such obedience? Most likely the raw convictions found in verses 5 and 8. In the former, Abraham had told his servants, 'I and the lad will go over there and worship and come back to you.' All those are first-person plural verbs—including 'we will come back to you.' Some expositors suggest Abraham was sort of covering up, so that the servants wouldn't get suspicious. But that is to forget that by this time Abraham had had a history with Yahweh and his faithfulness. He had seen him bring life out of the deadness of Sarah's womb. Somehow, he must have inferred, Yahweh can be trusted with this one. Hebrews 11:19 explains, 'Abraham reasoned that God could raise the dead' (NIV). And Abraham's words in verse 8 support this. Isaac had gone down the check-list. Fire. Wood. Then the haunting question: 'But where is the lamb?' (v. 7). (Had the two servants wondered about that too?) Abraham's comeback is, '*God* [emphatic subject] will see to it, the lamb, for a burnt-offering, my son' (v. 8). That's quite a literal translation; the sentence is choppy, perhaps reflecting the tension of the moment. The verb is often translated 'provide,' and that is fine; it's the verb 'to see,' and can have the sense of 'provide'; but 'see to it' captures the idea nicely here.

I recall speaking with a friend about a problem he and his wife were facing in their family. It was something that deeply concerned them, and they had often been in prayer about it. But near the end of our discussion, he simply said, 'Oh well, the Lord knows all about it.' That was not a cop-out; he was not expressing indifference or being flippant. Rather he was taking an Abraham-position. It was his way of saying that it was all in God's hands and he would 'see to it.'

Derek Kidner says that Abraham's response combines complete certainty about God with complete openness as to detail. In other words, he is sure of God; he is not sure of God's method. So the two men plod on. I can't help but imagine that the question of 18:25 still anchors Abraham—'Shall not the Judge of all the earth do right?' Even here. Abraham seems to assume that though God seems absurd, he will prove consistent; though he is baffling, he is nevertheless trustworthy; though he is mysterious, he is righteous. That's a pathway some of us will have to walk. Maybe some of us already have.

Thirdly, let us note **the relief of God's provision** in verses 9-14. Of course, there is no relief in verses 9-10, where the camera zooms in on every detail and those seven verbs slowly itemize every movement:

> ⁹Then they came to the place which God had designated to him. And Abraham built there an altar, arranged the wood in order, then bound Isaac his son, and placed him on the altar on top of the wood. ¹⁰And Abraham stretched out his hand and took hold of the knife to slay his son.

It's almost as if the narrative is dragging its feet and doesn't want to get to the breaking point until it must. But then heaven intervenes (v. 11) and is satisfied: 'You have not held back your son, your only one, from me' (v. 12). The sacrifice was essentially made and so the actual demand was withdrawn.

And here we see God's provision, first in the provision of a substitute (v. 13): 'there was a ram, behind him, caught in the thicket by his horns.' We must pay attention to this. Folks can get into trouble here when they are so intent on finding parallels between Isaac and Christ, when they try to make Isaac as the 'only son' into a type of Christ. He is not a foreshadowing of Christ but he is Abraham's seed—if anything he represents Israel. Isaac is the one who *receives* a substitute and must therefore need one—even Abraham's son, even Israel, needs a substitute. Even Presbyterians and Anglicans.

But then we can also see the provision of a pattern (v. 14). Victor Hamilton wants us to note that the place is not called 'Abraham obeyed' but 'Yahweh provides.' Or, if we pick up on our translation of verse 8 (the same verb is here in verse 14), the name is 'Yahweh will see (to it).' The rest of the verse is a bit tricky; it provides a further wordplay on the verb 'to see/provide' by using it in a sort of passive mode. The idea seems to be that this account of Yahweh's provision for Abraham caused folks to commemorate the event in subsequent days by saying, 'In the mountain of Yahweh it will be seen,' or, as Derek Kidner prefers to render it, 'In the mountain of Yahweh it will come clear.' The saying may contain a testimony, as if God's people are saying that when they worship Yahweh ('in the mountain of Yahweh'; Sinai? Zion?) they find that Yahweh acts toward them in an Abraham-kind-of-way—he provides or sees to it or makes it clear. What Yahweh did for Abraham depicts a tendency he exercises toward his people, who in their troubles find again and again that he is the God who sees to it.

We may have a sample of this sort of thing in Psalm 73. There Asaph is nearly undone as he wraps himself up in the way the wicked prosper while the righteous seem to get pounded into the ground; he almost threw in the towel on his faith. Then he says: 'Now when I tried to think this through, it was sheer turmoil to me, until I came into the sanctuary of God, then I began to understand their end' (vv. 16-17). Until I came into the sanctuary of God. A trip to the mountain of Yahweh. Then it came clear. It can be a bit strange how that happens.

I have always enjoyed the story Martyn Lloyd-Jones told (in *Healing and the Scriptures*) of preaching in a certain place and seeing, during the singing of one of the hymns, a man being brought in and practically carried by two friends. This man was a minister in the town and Lloyd-Jones had known him for some time. But he was obviously severely afflicted with rheumatoid arthritis. After the service the man sought Lloyd-Jones' advice. He had been able to get a bed at the Royal Mineral Hospital at Bath and wanted to go there for treatment. But then he had been told that he would only be admitted there if he were vaccinated; this worried him, for he was afraid that in his frail condition such a procedure might kill him. What was 'the Doctor's advice?' Lloyd-Jones told him that if he had been fortunate enough to get admission to that famous hospital, he should go at all costs. Apparently even if it killed him! Then Lloyd-Jones added, just as a kind of after-thought, 'Yes, and in any case you never know what good this vaccination may do you. It may very well clear up your whole condition.' It was left at that. Lloyd-Jones did not see the man for some six months, but when he did, the fellow was walking toward Lloyd-Jones and perfectly well. Lloyd-Jones said something about their obviously having fine treatment at Bath. The man told him that he had never gone there: 'As you said, I had such a violent reaction to the vaccination that it seemed to cure me.' And it had. But totally unexpected.

And sometimes that's what you find in public worship, in the 'mountain of the Lord.' That mountain of the Lord may be in a lovely traditional 'sanctuary' or among folding chairs in a middle school gymnasium. But there's a strange chemistry in public worship. There often beat up people come dragging their 'baggage' in (as they should—where else should they take it?) and find that Yahweh 'sees to it.' It is when they go into the sanctuary of God that they find this unexpected provision. Often adoring God will lift more of your burdens than understanding your burdens.

Lastly, we need to notice how verses 15-24 underscore **the insignificance of God's people**. And in the first segment, verses 15-19, we hear the promise in all its emphasis. The promise to Abraham is repeated but with greater certainty, clarity, and content. For this last, note the addition in verse 17b of 'and your seed will possess the gate of his enemies.' And all this because of Abraham's obedience (vv. 16, 18); obedience did matter; obedience does matter.

But then in the next segment, verses 20-24, we face the reality in all its starkness. Well, that may not be your first reaction. You may read these verses and simply think how dismal they are:

[20]After these things someone told Abraham, 'Look, Milcah—she also has given birth to sons to Nahor, your

brother: [21]Uz, his first-born, and Buz, his brother—and Kemuel, the father of Aram, [22]and Chesed, and Hazo, and Pildash, and Jidlaph, and Bethuel.' [23]Now Bethuel fathered Rebekah; Milcah gave birth to these eight (sons) to Nahor the brother of Abraham. [24]And his concubine—her name was Reumah—she also gave birth to Tebach and Gaham and Tahash and Maacah.

The story of the near sacrifice was scary, but at least it was gripping—but this material seems to bring on the yawns. Could we not sweep it under the rug? Some say this section is here because it introduces Rebekah (v. 23), which they say is necessary in some way. But no, that's not it. Don't you see it? Do the math. You have one son who is the survivor; you have Isaac versus these twelve in the non-covenant line. Almost nothing versus massive fertility. This is telling us that Nahor's clan isn't scratching along with one, single, measly son who almost got sacrificed! But God's chosen people appear fragile, few, flimsy, and unimpressive beside the vigorous growth and strength of the non-promise line. Let that picture sink in: God's people so often seem weak and nondescript over against the success and achievement and power of the world around them. They are 'mustard seed' stuff. They can look like a pretty hopeless bunch of folks.

So...don't get overly worried when Christ's people in the world don't seem to be dominant or flourishing or recognized or esteemed or tremendously significant. Their insignificance is often par for God's course. But God will see to it.

Well, God tested Abraham, and Abraham passed the test. One senses the sheer delight of heaven when the angel of Yahweh exclaims, 'You have not held back your son, your only one, from me' (v. 12). That verb, 'held back,' may have triggered Paul's thinking, for he used it in Romans 8:32 (and his is the same Greek verb as the Greek translation of the Old Testament used when it translated Genesis 22:12 200 years before Paul): *He who did not hold back his very own Son but handed him over for us all, how shall he not also—with him—freely give us all things?* What God kept Abraham from doing, he himself did!

A few years ago *Christian History* magazine told of a time when Martin Luther read this story in Genesis 22 for family devotions. When he had finished, his wife Katie exclaimed, 'I do not believe it. God would not have treated his son like that.' Then Luther turned to her and said, 'But Katie…he did!'

15

PROMISE BU$INE$$
(Genesis 23)

Apologies to readers in the UK and other countries who use other currencies than the US dollar—the dollar sign works for every 's' in the word 'business' in a way that the pound sterling sign doesn't. But to the point—what are we to make of this story? Why is it here? Proposed answers may depend on one's point of view. An attorney or solicitor may tell us that the Abraham-Ephron deal seemed to be carried out very carefully, specifying witnesses and terms (see verses 10, 11, 16, 17-18) and yet it is always wise to get professional help in such cases. If they ever read it, I suppose the funeral directors and morticians would be the ones who would go through the roof. They might say, 'Here's a clear sample of how not to do it. This is why we keep telling you via commercials and tele-marketing to pre-plan your funerals. Don't wait till the last moments when you have to make decisions under the pressure of time and the stress of grief.' Or think of a real estate agent. He or she would likely say, 'If Abraham had used a certified agency, he'd have gotten a better purchase price—everyone knows one never agrees to the initial asking price.' We can understand such viewpoints (and we wish each of these friends a good day at the office), but we are pretty sure that this passage is not here to tell us how to conduct business with an enclave of Hittites. We can usually assume that the story is here to instruct the people of God, but what does it mean to underscore? So, as in all our Bible reading, we come asking what we find here, what we are to hear, what we should see in this text.

We meet, first, **a common sorrow of covenant people** in verses 1 and 2:

> [1]Now the life of Sarah came to 127 years—the years of the life of Sarah. [2]So Sarah died in Kiriath-arba, that is Hebron, in the land of Canaan; and Abraham went in to mourn for Sarah and to weep over her.

This may be a 'common' sorrow but there is nothing common about this death. It is a special death. Sarah is the only woman in Genesis whose age is given at death. And Sarah is, in one sense, the mother of the people of God in this world. And yet for all that there is something common about this death. For Abraham, it is what we might call an 'ordinary' trial as compared to the severe test he endured in chapter 22. This at least is one of the trials that you expect to meet. To be sure, Abraham is a 'special' person, the funnel of redemption (12:1-3), and yet the last of verse 2 shows that he nevertheless endures common sorrows—one that every Tom, Dick, Harry, Marsha and Heather endure.

So Abraham here reminds us that God's covenant people are not sticks and stones, impervious to grief and sadness. We are not some sort of elite humanity that doesn't face these ravages. You may say: Well, yes, but we face them with triumph and victory. Well, maybe; often that is the case. But sometimes our losses are so sad, so distressing, so lonely that even as Christians we can't feel much of the 'victorious' element. Just because you're a Christian does not mean you don't mourn and weep over your loss, over the spouse who's no longer at your side or the child who no longer sits on your knee. And sometimes it may come in waves.

I was struck by this when reading the life of Charles Hodge, the well-known nineteenth century theology professor at old Princeton Seminary. His parents married about 1790 and were living in Philadelphia. They had three children in the next several years. But Elizabeth was taken away by yellow fever before she was three years old, and Mary and her younger brother sickened and died from measles in about two more years. In the latter two cases, Mrs Hodge had been away visiting her relatives and, upon hearing of her children's danger, hurried home, only to find Mary already dead and her brother near death. The Hodges had two more children, Hugh and Charles, but when Charles was six months old, his father died. His mother was left a widow, with a toddler and an infant. This was hardly an unusual scenario at that time, I'm sure, but it's still passing sad and devastating. There was grief on top of grief—and that packed into a short slice of time. Covenant people, to be sure, but with gobs of common sorrow.

Nor does it cease after death's formalities. For months and months the ache never leaves. Much, much later you may sense you're getting a handle on it, and then while you're standing in morning worship one Sunday singing *My Hope Is Built on Nothing Less* something sneaks up on you and turns on the water-works. Does faith make a difference? Of course, it does, but faith doesn't insulate you from sorrow—in fact, the deeper the love, the closer the relation, the more severe the grief may be. 'Abraham went in to mourn for Sarah and to weep over her.'

We meet, secondly, in this text **a clear confession of pilgrim status** (vv. 3-6). In spite of the fact that locals regard Abraham as 'a mighty prince' (lit., 'a prince of God,' v. 6) and in spite of the fact that he packed some wallop with his wealth and influence, still, in the wake of Sarah's death and his need for a burial plot, he knows all too clearly his current status: 'I am a sojourner and stranger among you' (v. 4; renderings vary among translations). 'Sojourner' here translates *ger* (gay-urr), an alien, one who didn't enjoy the rights of a resident, one who had abandoned his homeland for political or economic reasons and sought refuge in another community; and 'stranger' renders *toshav*, one who has no land of his own but is settled upon that of another, a sort of tenant. Hebrews 11:13 picks up this description; it says that Abraham and Co. acknowledged that 'they were strangers and exiles on the earth' (ESV). Abraham had no spot to call his own.

But the Bible wants all of God's people to realize that they are in an Abraham position. In Leviticus 25:23 Yahweh told Israel how they were to think of themselves once they were in the land: 'For the land is mine; for you are sojourners and strangers with me.' David, in face of the fragility of life, confesses to Yahweh, 'For I am a sojourner with you, a guest [*toshav*], like all my fathers' (Ps. 39:12 ESV). When the apostle Peter begins his chunk of exhortation in 1 Peter 2:11–3:12, he starts by addressing his readers in Genesis 23:4 lingo: 'I urge you as sojourners and exiles to abstain from the passions of the flesh' (2:11 ESV). That is the way we are to think of ourselves in this world.

Sometimes this demand may come home with special force, even irony. A. M. Hunter (in *Probing the New Testament*) tells of Karl Ludwig Schmidt, a New Testament professor in Germany, who was to contribute the article on *paroikos* (Greek for 'sojourner') for what became in English the *Theological Dictionary of the New Testament*. This is a work of ten thick volumes, with peacock-blue binding. The original 'Dictionary' began to appear in the early 1930s, a time when Schmidt had leveled criticism against the Nazi regime. Nazis never cared for criticism and so they deposed him from his university chair in Bonn, expelled him from the 'fatherland,' and took his citizenship away. So Schmidt finished the article on *paroikos* for the Dictionary after he had himself become one—in Switzerland. And in the present hour how very many Syrian and Iraqi Christians know what it is to be literally 'sojourners and strangers' because of the butchers of the Islamic State.

We must ponder this matter. There is a sense in which we must stand in the sandals of Abraham, confessing that we are sojourners and pilgrims. You must never forget who you are, how fragile and rootless and utterly dependent on God—and sitting loose to this age and all that it holds and offers. There is a certain and proper detachment that should mark us. Sometimes grief or loss or reversals can bring this mindset home with fresh force. Sometimes getting that right perspective again is strangely comforting and reassuring. I find that sense of 're-set' in a story Richard Bewes tells (*Words that Circled the World*). He says that years ago Boris Becker was on the victim end of an upset win at Wimbledon. So—not unexpectedly— the TV interviewer in the post-match assessment asked him, 'What went wrong?' The blue eyes, Bewes says, opened wide in surprise. '*Wrong?* Nothing has gone wrong. Nobody has died! I lost at tennis, right?'

It was not a catastrophe but a tennis loss. Sometimes it takes a disciplined outlook to see it for what it is. That's the way sojourners and strangers look at things. It's not that they don't have any emotions or ambitions; but they do seem to have a holy indifference about their 'stuff,' a godly flexibility about the twists and turns their lives take, a sanctified nonchalance over making their mark. But none of it matters as long as we can say with David, to Yahweh, 'I am a sojourner **with you**' (ESV).

Lastly, we must see here **a small sign of God's faithfulness** (vv. 7-20). Now you can miss the 'small sign' by simply enjoying the story too much! One has to admit that the give-and-take of the business deal in verses 5-16 is fascinating: the locals offer Abraham the use of a 'borrowed' burial plot (v. 6); Abraham makes a counter-proposal, asking to deal with Ephron to make a deal for the cave of Machpelah at the end of his field 'for full payment in silver' (vv. 7-9); one notes the constant references to witnesses (vv. 10, 11, 13, 16, 18)—all the legal requirements are carefully met; Ephron makes his own counter-offer—he will sell both the field and the cave to Abraham (v. 11). Now why did Ephron do that? Who can tell? Did he want to bring in more cash? Did he want out from under tax liability for the field? In any case, it is field-plus-cave. Abraham's acceptance of the proposal is a bit difficult to translate ('If only you…O that you would listen to me: I give the silver for the field; take it from me, and let me bury my dead there,' v. 13), but clearly he agrees to Ephron's bargain. What about the price? 'Price,' Ephron seems to say in verse 15, 'did someone say "price"?' 'Land worth 400 weight of silver—what is that between me and you?' (v. 15). That was probably a fairly stiff price—Ephron did have Abraham over a barrel, but the latter paid up (v. 16). It's all a fascinating bit of Middle Eastern wheeling and dealing.

But what's *really* going on? Behind all the silver and witnesses and caves and trees? Well, note verses 2 and 19, at the beginning and at the end of the story. Notice that each of these verses refer to Hebron and then adds, 'in the land of Canaan.' That jogs our memories about 12:5, when Abraham and company came 'into the land of Canaan' and then Yahweh said to him 'To your seed I will give this land' (12:7). So chapter 23 is connected especially to the place-aspect of Yahweh's promise. And here, as he obtains a cemetery plot for Sarah, he gets a 'possession' (used three times, vv. 4, 9, 20, plus a synonym in verse 18, which we may translate 'acquisition') in the land. A miniscule chunk of Canaan is now his! This field and cave where Sarah is buried is *in the land*—it is a tiny bit of land in the land God promised, a mere parcel of what Yahweh promised. But it *is* a bit! Yahweh's promise of the land has *begun* to come true. It is, to be sure, a small—but real—encouragement.

And something small can prove a huge encouragement. In one of his books Ron Enroth tells of Bryan and Cyndi, who had made the break from a very dictatorial and oppressive church group. So concerned were they that they moved away from the very vicinity where the church was; they moved to St Louis, even though it meant Bryan would not have a job there for some time. It was a difficult period, and yet Cyndi testifies that God's provision never failed. She tells of one hot summer day when she was recovering from the flu and wanted some orange juice. But they couldn't afford any. She and Bryan were walking down Grand Avenue in St Louis, apparently in the middle of the afternoon that day. No one else was in sight. A can of frozen orange juice came rolling down the sidewalk. Still with frost on its sides! They looked to see who it could belong to, but could find no one. So Bryan turned to her and said, 'Honey, I think it's for you.' Pretty small stuff. It's only a can of orange juice. But for them a big sign of the kindness of God!

That is what Abraham finds here—a small sign of God's faithfulness. Perhaps we can put a spin on Luke 16:10 and say that Yahweh is the God who is 'faithful in little.' And it is easy to miss seeing such mercy-drops. Haven't you often found that Yahweh takes this way with you? There is not necessarily the total relief or the complete solution, but there is the tiny token, the small assurance, that God gives in the midst of our sorrows and sadnesses, at just the time we need it.

What we have here in Genesis 23 does not look promising; indeed, it may look like Abraham is trying to play a hopeless game of catch-up. It reminds me of a story Michael Medved told of his university days when he would hitchhike all over the country. He once managed to get a ride with a burly, tattooed truck driver along the Ohio turnpike. As they drove along, the trucker popped a tape into his tape deck and began to play the Schubert 'Symphony in C Major.' Medved recognized the music and it led into a two-hour conversation of the comparative virtues of Schubert and Beethoven. The trucker had never finished high school, but he owned his own home, sent his two kids to a parochial school, and saved money to buy tickets to the Cleveland Orchestra. Who would think one would discuss Schubert with a trucker with colored ink dribbled down his arms? That's Genesis 23. It doesn't look like much, but it tells us that God has already begun to fulfill his promise, if only with a 'small' faithfulness. In what may appear to be the most barren parts of Scripture, the Holy Spirit awaits you, to teach and instruct you, that the word of Christ may dwell in you richly.

16

COVENANT ROMANCE
(Genesis 24)

What if you want to lead a Bible study for your youth group on finding a life's mate and you use Genesis 24 and call it 'Guidance and Girls'? And you tell them: (1) put yourself in a place where you'll meet fellows or girls (v. 11); (2) commit the matter to prayer (vv. 12-13); (3) make your prayer specific (v. 14)—too many of our prayers are generalizations; (4) don't forget to give thanks (vv. 26-27); and (5) you need to meet the family (vv. 28-51), not that you marry them but they can tell you a lot about the person you do hope to marry. Now that we know how *not* to interpret Genesis 24, we can proceed ahead. What's it about? About God's promise program for the nations (12:1-3) meeting another glitch. Yahweh intends to bring his kingdom into this world through Abraham's seed, and, finally, Abraham has that seed—Isaac. But the problem is that the seed needs seed, and the seed won't get seed if he doesn't get married (or so it was then). Yahweh's promise-plan seems to lurch along by a bunch of stutters and stops, hindrances here and roadblocks there. And it will come to a dead end if Isaac doesn't first of all get a wife. Hence this story of covenant romance. And so we have to ask: what does this covenant romance teach us?

First, it teaches us that **God's promises require faithful activity** (vv. 1-9). Abraham laid on his servant two non-negotiable requirements: he must not take a wife for Isaac from the Canaanites (v. 3) and he must not take Isaac back to Abraham's former homeland (v. 6). Verse 7 sums up Abraham's faith in the matter, as if in answer to all the 'what-ifs' that could be raised: 'Yahweh…will send his angel before you and you will take a wife for my son from there.' Certainly the land promise meant that Abraham's seed was to stay in Canaan (see v. 7), but a wretched marriage would sabotage the covenant (hence no Canaanite girls). Abraham likely knew that the Canaanites were to come under judgment (see 15:16; cf. 9:25-27). Seeking Isaac's wife 'back home' was a costly decision for Abraham, no doubt, because he would likely have profited handsomely, both economically and militarily, by making a marriage alliance with some powerful Canaanite chieftain. It's not that Abraham's kin were faithful Yahweh worshipers but they seemed to practice 'light' paganism compared to the gross paganism of the Canaanites (cf. Leviticus 18 for the latter).

Verses 1-9 recognize that marriage is essential for covenant continuity, but they also seem to recognize that a wrong-headed marriage can destroy covenant fidelity. That seems to be a sort of suppressed worry in Abraham's instructions (v. 3). All this becomes more explicit later when Israel is about to enter the land—they must not intermarry with pagans in the land because it will lead to apostasy (Deut. 7:3-4). Marriage matters in the covenant; indeed, holy marriages are essential for ongoing covenant fidelity. This same concern seems behind Paul's directions to Christian widows in 1 Corinthians 7:39; if such a woman's husband dies she is free to remarry whomever she wants—'only in the Lord.'

That's all well and good: if you are bound to Christ by covenant, you must only marry someone who is also one of Christ's covenant people. But what if—to take it from the fellow's viewpoint—there's no 'Rebekah'? What if in the providence of God no Christian girl ever comes across the radar screen of your life as a viable candidate? What then?

There is an interesting snip in Ned Stonehouse's biography of Gresham Machen. Machen was New Testament professor at Princeton Seminary and later taught at and led Westminster Seminary. But at one point Machen was apparently quite serious with a lady from Boston. She was said to be 'intelligent, beautiful, exquisite'—a hard combination to beat. They were quite devoted to each other for a time, though the relationship never blossomed into an engagement. The reason was that she was a Unitarian. She apparently made a real effort to believe but could not bring her mind to a point where she could share Machen's Christian faith. Machen, on his part, could not think of uniting his life to one who could not share basic agreement with him regarding his faith. So the relationship was ended. That is hard. Sometimes faithfulness may require that, however. Marriage matters. The wrong kind can sabotage covenant faithfulness for years to come.

Secondly, this covenant romance teaches us that **God's providence maintains God's purposes** (vv. 10-61). This is a huge chunk of narrative and we will have to summarize. Note how all of a sudden Abraham's servant is there: 'so he rose and went to Aram-naharaim, to the city of Nahor' (v. 10b). As often, the Bible spares you the details of the trip, so as to focus on the main drama of God's providence, which is what we might call the 'execution factor' in working out God's purposes. Abraham's purpose and, it seems, God's purpose is to find a wife for Isaac, and that purpose will be brought about via the working of God's interesting providence.

One matter we must note is that sometimes minor characters may play major roles in God's providence. Abraham's servant is in one sense a 'minor character', but of course he dominates this section of the story. Notice how much 'press' he gets;

notice his extended speech in verses 34-49. He is really a model servant (see vv. 12-14, 26-27, 52), and seems to display just the right kind of gracious and godly 'pushiness' throughout. How good God is to give Abraham such a faithful, godly servant! How much rests on this one man. That is often the case in God's dramas.

General Robert E. Lee was quite closed-mouth about re-living battles of the War between the States. But Shelby Foote tells of a time when, post-war, Lee was out riding with a friend and permitted himself a brief reflection. 'If I had had Stonewall Jackson with me,' he said, 'so far as man can see, I should have won the battle of Gettysburg.' To Lee, one man could have made all the difference.

Yet Abraham's servant is no Stonewall, in that he does not even have a name. Some may assume he is the same as Eliezer of chapter 15, but that is not necessarily the case. We do not know. Don't you often find this to be the case—that God uses ordinary 'no-name' sort of people to work good for you? The God of the Bible is not dependent on all-stars.

But more than this we must notice the simply interesting development of God's providence. The servant's recipe seems to be to mix circumstances (v. 11) with prayer (vv. 12-14) and see what happens. And it is intriguing to note that Yahweh never speaks in the story, though he is often mentioned by others. In his prayer the servant had proposed a rather revealing test for the girl—that she would not only give him a drink but then, voluntarily, offer to water all the servant's camels (v. 14). I can't help it—one of those 'what-if' moments strikes me here. What if Rebekah was cast in a twenty-first century mold, came to the well chomping a wad of gum and with the habit of using the word 'like' promiscuously? She might say, 'Yeah, okay, like you asked for a drink and that's like cool, but don't expect any more. Like those camels drink liters and liters and if I like messed with them, I'd like be here all evening. Besides, just while I've been like getting water, I've had like two texts on my phone and I want to like answer them.' We can be thankful that, like, Rebekah was not like that.

Rather, Rebekah seems to vigorously fulfill the servant's test in verses 18-20—and it was a real revelation of her character. We know that a camel drinks something like twenty-five gallons of water to replenish the amount of weight it has lost and, according to Nahum Sarna, it takes ten minutes for it to drink this amount. A normal water jar at the time might have a capacity of three gallons (Walton), so a three-gallon jar and ten camels (see v. 10) at twenty-five gallons a piece and that girl is flitting back and forth from well to trough some eighty to a hundred times. This woman is not allergic to work. And…she's from Abraham's family (v. 24). When Laban and Bethuel hear the servant's account of his prayer and Rebekah's precise fulfillment of it, they can only acknowledge that this is Yahweh's doing (v. 50).

This sort of fascinating providence is not merely back-there-in-Bible-times stuff. Fact is, Christian history and biography and experience are chocked full of such delightful samples of God's providence. We run into it again and again; one is tempted to say it is typical of God. Sometimes there is a long chain of providences before one sees the end-product. I think of one of Faith Cook's mini-biographies of the Saphir family (in *Singing in the Fire*), of the way Israel (the father) and Adolph (the son) came to faith in Jesus as the Messiah. About 1838 the Church of Scotland sent a delegation on a fact-finding trip to scout out evangelistic opportunities among Jews in the Middle East and Europe. One of the men, Dr Keith, became very sleepy while going through the Sinai desert and fell off his camel. The injury proved far more serious than at first thought, so Drs Keith and Black were to return to Scotland. Contrary to their original plans, they decided to return via the Danube River and rest a few days in Pesth. But they were detained far longer because both of them became ill with Danube fever; Keith collapsed in the street and was in a coma for six weeks, while Black was in the adjacent room, helpless to help his friend. The Archduchess, who apparently had quietly come to faith, aided these men in their illness and asked them to return to work among the people. After they had returned, in 1841 the church sent Dr John Duncan to Pesth. Ministry was difficult in a Roman Catholic country, but there were English workmen in the city and services could be held for them. Some Jews began attending these services, among them Israel Saphir and his eleven-year-old son, Adolph. Mr Saphir was the most learned Jew in Hungary and highly respected. At first he attended apparently to better his English, but then, via conversations with Dr Duncan and being a part of the worship, father and son came to believe. All finally became known one day when son Adolph, while giving thanks for their meal, closed his prayer 'in the name of Jesus.' Now in one sense that does not seem very remarkable at all and in another it is most remarkable—what a chain of un-inventible events! Might you imagine asking Adolph Saphir in a few years how he came to faith in Christ? Mightn't he begin with, 'Well, it all started when a Scotsman fell off his camel in Palestine…'

Whether it's Genesis 24 or myriads of other samples we are simply left asking ourselves, 'Isn't God fascinating? Aren't his ways delightful?' But then we would short-circuit things if we left them there. We must not simply ask *ourselves* these questions but make them declarations to *God*. We must follow the lead of Abraham's servant and get lost in wonder, love, and praise for such work:

> Then the man bowed down and worshiped Yahweh. And he said: 'How blessed is Yahweh, God of my master Abraham, who has not forsaken his steadfast love and faithfulness with my master! As for me, Yahweh led

me on the road to the house of my master's brothers'
(vv. 26-27).

When Abraham's servant heard their words, he bowed
to the ground before Yahweh [v. 52].

He offers worship, both after the circumstances played out
(vv. 26-27) and after consent had been given (v. 52). Isn't that
the only response we can give to this God who shows us later
that he has been silently there all the time, working perhaps
with people, times, reactions, and circumstances we could
never have dreamed?

Then, finally, this covenant romance teaches us that **God's
provision satisfies his servants** (vv. 62-67). Now we're back in
Canaan. We don't know exactly how to translate verse 63, but
perhaps Isaac was meditating in the field toward evening—and
he catches sight of the camels! And Rebekah finds out who
it is who is coming to meet them (vv. 64-65). Then verse 67
wraps it all up:

And Isaac brought her into the tent of Sarah his mother.
And he took Rebekah, and she became his wife—and
he loved her. So Isaac was comforted after his mother's
death.

What is at stake here in Isaac's getting his wife? Why, the whole
promise- and kingdom-plan of God. There will be no people
of God in this world if Isaac doesn't marry and start having
kids. But what else does the text show us? Did you hear the last
line of verse 67? The story isn't only about Yahweh's plan but
about human need. Isaac is not a mere cog in God's plan for
the world, but he is a hurting person for whom God cares. And
why does he hurt? He misses his mother. He aches because
of her death and absence. There may well have been a very

close bond between Isaac and Sarah. So what does God do? He gave Isaac someone to love, a wife, Rebekah. And someone to love him back. Yahweh stooped down to begin to fill up the hole in Isaac's life. Yahweh is the God of the big plan and of the individual need. The huge emotional vacuum in Isaac's life mattered to Yahweh. When you are among the covenant people of God you are not lost in a massive crowd; Yahweh always sees his individual servants. Paul Gerhardt captures all this in one of his hymns:

> *Commit now all your griefs*
> *and ways into his hands;*
> *to his sure truth and tender care,*
> *who earth and heav'n commands.*
> *Who points the clouds their course,*
> *whom winds and seas obey,*
> *he shall direct your wand'ring feet,*
> *he shall prepare your way.*
>
> *Give to the winds your fears;*
> *hope, and be undismayed;*
> *God hears your sighs and counts your tears,*
> *God shall lift up your head…*

So this is the story of covenant romance. It's a beautiful story—it reflects the beauty of Yahweh our God.

17

Sunset
(Genesis 25:1-18)

It wouldn't seem to hold much interest for a small lad. 'It' was the two-car garage behind the United Presbyterian manse in our small Pennsylvania town. My father's old Chevrolet was usually in it, in the mornings at least, and there were other items like garden tools and a wheelbarrow and gasoline drums and, in the fall, a bushel or so of Northern Spy apples. But as a six to eight-year-old I had to make a good bit of my own fun and much of it took place in this garage. For I could open the trunk (boot) of the Chevy and get the scissors jack out; I knew where to place it if I wanted to jack up a rear wheel of the car and where to put it if I wanted to jack up a front wheel. I knew how to open the hood (U.K.: bonnet) and look around there; the right rear hubcap was a bit different and I was able to pry it off with a screwdriver. I wasn't strong enough to loosen the lug nuts on the tires, fortunately. My father had made a home-made 'creeper' on casters, so that he could crawl under the car more conveniently. I would make use of that—jack up a front wheel and then get on the creeper and shoot myself under the car. (My parents were rather strict, so why they allowed me to fool around like this I don't know—maybe they had life insurance on me that I didn't know about!). In any case, I could play mechanic to my heart's content. And what looked rather prosaic and dull on the surface was, after all, a source of immense enjoyment for me.

Now there are gobs of biblical texts like that. To the superficial glance they look dull, mundane at best, and utterly uninviting—and yet they may hide surprising treasure. Like this passage relating the 'sunset' of Abraham's life. Check it out for yourself:

> Now Abraham again took a wife—and her name was Keturah. ²And she bore to him Zimran and Jokshan and Medan and Midian and Ishbak and Shuah; ³and Jokshan fathered Sheba and Dedan, and the sons of Dedan were Asshurim and Letushim and Leummim. ⁴And the sons of Midian were: Ephah and Epher and Hanoch and Abida and Eldaah. All these were sons of Keturah.

Not a very scintillating or titillating start. The whole passage is nothing but obituaries and genealogies and yet—typical for the Bible—these teach theology. The writer doesn't want you to get away until you understand why you should care about Mibsam, Mishma, and Massa. So, once more, what does this text teach us? It teaches us, first, that **God's bright faithfulness often appears in plain packages**.

However, before we support this point perhaps we should address the problem of Keturah in verses 1-4. The text only tells you now about Keturah, though it may well be that Abraham took her as his wife much earlier. If Abraham seemed to think he was pro-creatively 'washed up' at 100 years of age (17:17), then one would hardly expect him to beget offspring like this after Sarah had died (ch. 23). Someone may ask: But what of God's design for marriage in 2:24, one man, one woman? That question raises another question: Do we ever allow culture rather than the word of God to direct our practices? Yes, though we may be blind to the fact. So we may need to go easy on throwing rocks at Abraham. In any case, there seem to be something like sixteen descendants by Keturah. And identifications are difficult, though some are possible. Midian was originally east of Aqaba in northwest Arabia; Ishbak may have been a north Syrian tribe; Sheba was in the southwest part of the Arabian peninsula, big in the spice trade; and Dedan in the northwestern part the same peninsula. But all Keturah's offspring was well provided for and shuffled off away from Isaac (vv. 5-6).

But where does Yahweh's faithfulness appear? If we simply keep tracking, we see some of it in verses 7-8: Abraham was 175 years old when he died 'in a good old age, old and contented' (v. 8). That is a fulfillment of Yahweh's word to him in 15:15 ('As for you, you will go to your fathers in peace; you will be buried in a good old age'). Or notice the burial notice in verses 9-10—Isaac and Ishmael buried Abraham 'in the cave of Machpelah in the field of Ephron son of Zohar the Hittite,' which was the field Abraham had purchased in order that he could bury Sarah. That conjures up the whole episode of chapter 23, where Yahweh first actually gave Abraham an actual chunk of Canaan, beginning to fulfill his place-promise. Then, the very mention of Beer-lahai-roi, where Isaac was staying, in verse 11 brings to mind God's care and kindness to Hagar in 16:13-14 (cf. 'the well of the living one who sees me'). And finally, the whole raft of Ishmael's descendants in verses 12-18 trumpets the faithfulness of God, because God had told Hagar that he would greatly multiply her seed (16:10-12), had assured Abraham that he would make Ishmael fruitful, indeed that he would father twelve leaders (17:20, and here, especially 25:16), and had promised Hagar that he would make Ishmael into a great nation (21:18). This last promise is beginning to be fulfilled here in verses 12-18.

There is much more than there appears to be in verses 7-18. It is something like Sherlock Holmes, who once was scrutinizing a man's pipe and divined that the fellow who used it was muscular, left-handed, with an excellent set of teeth, careless in his habits, and with no need to practice economy. The remnants of the tobacco in the pipe were of a high-priced brand, one far above what would be a very adequate 'smoke' and so the fellow could freely spend what he wanted. Because it was charred down the right side it was clear that the smoker was used to lighting it at lamps or gas jets and so he must be left-handed. And since he had bitten through his amber, he must be a fairly muscular fellow with a good set of teeth. Simply look over a man's pipe and find out all that!

That's the way it is in verses 7-18: pick them apart and you see all sorts of traces of God's faithfulness to his word. These are not of the razzle-dazzle sort; you have to dig them out and think them through. They are very low-key. It's nothing like Abraham's gall bladder being miraculously healed or Sarah's sciatica suddenly disappearing. God wraps a lot of his faithfulness in plain brown packages. But if you can appreciate this text, if you can 'sherlock' it, you realize it is loaded with divine assurances. And this should tell you that you don't need sensational signs and wonders and racy testimonies and ranting televangelists; you don't need super-signs, because you have Ishmael's genealogy and Hagar's well and the cave of Machpelah, and you can run with that. And if your Lord is completely reliable in these matters, then surely he can be trusted to fulfill his assurances in John 6:37 and 10:28.

This text teaches us, secondly, that **God gives a flicker of hope even in our obituaries** (vv. 7-10). Notice especially verses 8-9a: 'Then Abraham breathed his last and died in a good old age, old and contented, and he was gathered to his people. So Isaac and Ishmael his sons buried him....' I want particularly to focus on 'he was gathered to his people' in verse 8.

This phraseology is used of Ishmael (v. 17), Isaac (35:29), Jacob (49:33), Aaron (Num. 20:24, 26), and Moses (Num. 27:13; 31:2; Deut. 32:50). This is not synonymous with death, for it seems to occur post-death (note v. 8). It is not the same as burial in an ancestral grave, because neither Abraham nor Aaron nor Moses was buried with their forefathers. Nor is it synonymous with burial, for verse 9 here seems to indicate that burial is distinct from it. Note, for example, how in 49:33 Jacob is 'gathered' but burial is maybe two months or more later (50:7).

What does 'gathered to his people' imply? Well, if Abraham, for example, is gathered to his people, it implies that 'his people' still exist in some way even though they are dead. Being 'gathered' to one's people implies that men and women 'survive' in some way and join their forebears in the realm of the dead. There is no room to build racy mythologies on this, as one sometimes, sadly, hears at funerals—about so-and-so enjoying parties and giving 'high-fives' to cousins. None of that. But the clause does intimate that death does not mean annihilation; when you die you do not cease to exist.

Why even bother with this? Because we've been told by much traditional Old Testament scholarship that the Israelite people were basically existential nincompoops who didn't concern themselves much about life after death until very, very late in their history. And yet here, early on, is an oh-by-the-way recognition of ongoing existence in the face of death, of— one could say—immortality. And likely more, as David says to Yahweh in Psalm 139:8, 'And if I should make my bed in Sheol [the realm of the dead], there you are!' Post-death you are not only 'gathered to your people' but also met by your God.

Of course, we must enter a qualification. Genesis 25:8 is not 1 Corinthians 15 or 1 Thessalonians 4:13-18, nor does it pack the punch that the last chapters of the four gospels do. Yet clearly there is a hint of hope here, and we should not neglect any hope that is ours. I've already tried to point out from Genesis 17 that Abraham himself must have assumed the resurrection of the dead. That is more than this 'gathered to his people' note tells us here, but even this little note tells us that death is not annihilation, that death is not the end for the people of God, and leads us to believe that we need not fear but that we will have God's care at such a time, for, as Psalm 116:15 says, 'Precious in the sight of Yahweh is the death of his saints.'

Once more, this text teaches us that **God's cause is not frustrated by our unavailability**. This is the clear import of verse 11: 'Now after the death of Abraham, God blessed Isaac his son; and Isaac stayed near Beer-lahai-roi.' This kind of expression ('after the death of so-and-so') does not occur elsewhere in Genesis-Deuteronomy, but it is used again in Joshua 1:1, Judges 1:1, and 2 Samuel 1:1, referring to the deaths of Moses, Joshua, and Saul respectively. In each case, as Nahum Sarna points out, it indicates a historical turning point and recognizes that an era has come to an end. But the expression also exudes an air of crisis as well. Think of the passages cited. Joshua 1 tells us that Moses has died. We may wonder if that is really the case since he's mentioned eleven times in Joshua 1. But what will happen now? There was no one like Moses (Deut. 34:10-12), in spite of the fact that Israel seemed to make life miserable for him most of the time. And what will happen in Israel once the bold military leadership of Joshua passes off the scene? And what can Israel expect with King Saul dead, Israel's army decimated, and the Philistines in control of a big chunk of northern Israel (1 Sam. 31)? These 'after the death of' words always seem to carry an overtone of anxiety and imply a worried question: How will matters go on from here?

Here, in Genesis 25, the answer is: Quite well, thank you! 'After the death of Abraham, *God blessed Isaac his son*.' To be sure, Isaac was no Abraham, but then nothing ultimately depended on Abraham anyway. Not even Abraham is indispensable.

God's servants die, God's promise-plan continues. The death of God's servant does not signal the end of God's cause.

That is not always the case in mere human situations. In *O Jerusalem!* Larry Collins and Dominique Lapierre tell of how the Israelis seized an outpost from the Arabs during the 1947–48 war. They had taken Kastel, a little west of Jerusalem. Kamal Irekat, who would lead the Arab counter-attack, sent his messengers through the villages to round up his fighters. He had some four hundred men to throw against the seventy Jewish defenders. Irekat's men swept the Jews from their trenches and forced them back into some quarry buildings. All night the fighting went on. By morning the Arabs received reinforcements; they drove the Israelis from the quarry buildings and even back to the outskirts of the village itself. But the attackers had to take breaks because they needed food and ammunition. This took some time. But by sunset they could renew the attack. A bit after midnight Irekat and his men were within hand-grenade range; but at this point Irekat himself was wounded. The only medic available treated him and then, over Irekat's violent protests, strapped him onto a mule for the trip back to Jerusalem. Why such protests? Because Irekat knew the psychology of his village fighters: they magnified the importance of the leader, looked upon him with a sort of cult-like devotion. Led by such a man, they were capable of great bravery, of amazing feats. Without his presence to galvanize them, they would rapidly disintegrate. As it happened. The Israelis were bracing for the final assault on their position, and then they saw the enemy wandering off the battlefield; the fighters were simply going back to their villages.

It is never like that in Yahweh's regime. Whether it's Abraham or Moses or whoever who goes, it never throws a kink into his purposes. And God doesn't need first-stringers; he's not dependent on a varsity squad. If he doesn't have an Abraham, he can make do with an Isaac. Nor does he need a pantheon of elite evangelical leaders. Just to think of North America, what would happen if the reformed and Presbyterian presence passed from the scene? What if groups and denominations like the ARP and the RPCNA and the PCA and the EPC and the OPC and the CRC and others all went belly up? What if the church in North America (or the U.K. or wherever) became wholly like its culture? Isaiah 45:23 would still come to pass. Isn't it wonderful that you do not have a god who depends on you? You do not have to prop up God and his cause because he is perfectly capable of handling all that himself. He is the Isaiah 46 God who holds *you* up and carries *you* (Isa. 46:3-4).

You may think reading genealogies rather dull and that reading obituaries is a grave experience, but they are likely to tell you more about God than you ever thought possible.

OTHER BOOKS OF INTEREST FROM

CHRISTIAN FOCUS PUBLICATIONS

the
W a y
o f t h e
Righteous
in the
Muck
of Life

Psalms 1-12

Dale Ralph Davis

ISBN 978-1-84550-581-3

The Way of the Righteous in the Muck of Life

Psalms 1-12

Dale Ralph Davis

In the opening pages of the Psalms, believers discover foundational truth for right living-and great delight – as children of God. Trusted theologian Dale Ralph Davis leads readers through a careful study of Psalms 1-12 with clear application for daily life.

The Psalmist begins with the most essential truth for mankind, Davis explains: "Nothing is so crucial as your belonging to the congregation of the righteous." And it is the Word of God that provides the direction for the believer's life. It is here, Davis points out, that "the righteous man gets his signals for living." The delight of the righteous is in the "law"-the teachings-of the Lord. Indeed, for those who belong to Him, meditating on God's Word is "the pursuit of pleasure"! The Psalms are a treasure trove for such a pursuit.

As the first 12 Psalms continue, we see basic principles unfold with great clarity. Much like our troubles today, the Psalmist endured wickedness all around, a world hostile to the true God-and on a very personal level-deceit and persecution from his enemies. Readers are pointed toward the glorious rule of the Messiah, to whom the whole world belongs. In light of this realization, we are prepared to face all kinds of troubles that cause despair. The righteous rely on God, and the Psalms teach us how. This book is ideal for use by small groups, as a teaching guide or for reference.

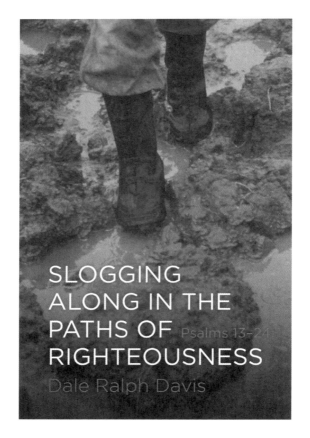

SLOGGING
ALONG IN THE
PATHS OF Psalms 13–24
RIGHTEOUSNESS

Dale Ralph Davis

ISBN 978-1-78191-304-8

Slogging Along the Paths of Righteousness

Psalms 13-24

Dale Ralph Davis

Dale Ralph Davis plunges right into the middle of King David's hard times with a study that is resonant for our lives. King David's faith brought him through the muddy parts of life. Will we find that depression is our final response to a hard path? Will faith carry us across?

Find the encouragement that Psalms 13-24 hold for the Scripture-filled life.

> Always fresh, always insightful. Dale Ralph Davis shows you what's there and leaves you wondering why you didn't see it before!
>
> COLIN S. SMITH,
> Senior Pastor, The Orchard, Arlington and President, Unlocking the Bible

> Dale Ralph Davis has provided another faithful, lively and refreshing set of expositions. All Christians will benefit from this book and I hope it is read widely.
>
> SAM ALLBERRY,
> Assistant Pastor, St Marys, Maidenhead and Author of *Is God Anti-Gay?*

> Dale Ralph Davis is among the finest expositors of the Old Testament alive today. His style is unique and his content infectious. A pastor at heart, his insights are always governed by an absolute loyalty to the text, a belief that the Bible was written for today as much as yesterday, and a desire to encourage his readers to fall in love with Scripture and to trust it.
>
> DEREK THOMAS,
> Senior Minister of Preaching and Teaching,
> First Presbyterian Church, Columbia, South Carolina

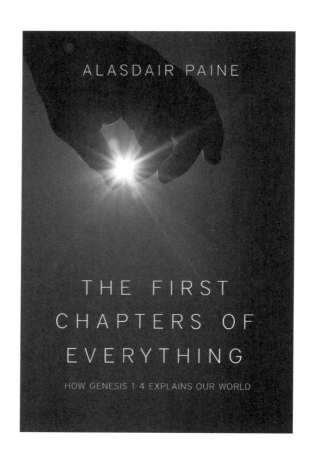

ALASDAIR PAINE

THE FIRST
CHAPTERS OF
EVERYTHING

HOW GENESIS 1-4 EXPLAINS OUR WORLD

ISBN 978-1-78191-323-9

First Chapters of Everything

How Genesis Chapters 1 to 4 Explains Our World

Alasdair Paine

Alasdair Paine writes in his introduction, "Genesis was not given to satisfy our speculation but to bring us urgent truths about God, our world and ourselves." This book was written to bring out the beginnings recorded in Genesis - where we came from, what went wrong, and the first promise of the Saviour to come.

> Deceptively clear and digestible style... He is preoccupied with 'What is God saying to us here?' and refuses to allow the elephant of secondary issues to stand between us and the Genesis text (though he provides additional notes for the curious). Here is a book I found refreshing my spirit, stimulating my mind, and nourishing my soul.
>
> DALE RALPH DAVIS,
> Minister in Residence, First Presbyterian Church, Columbia, South Carolina

> There is no better brief introduction to Genesis 1-4 than this. Alasdair Paine helpfully engages with the complex questions of interpretation but never gets bogged down... The focus throughout is God's contemporary message to us through these chapters, which is presented with great clarity and powerful application.
>
> VAUGHAN ROBERTS,
> Rector of St Ebbe's, Oxford and Director of Proclamation Trust

> ... devotionally engaging and stirring as well as useful for thinking how I might preach these important chapters. I've done that on a number of occasions, but this book made me want to do it again...
>
> ADRIAN REYNOLDS,
> Director of Ministry, The Proclamation Trust

DALE RALPH DAVIS

THE WORD
BECAME FRESH

HOW TO PREACH FROM OLD TESTAMENT NARRATIVE TEXTS

ISBN 978-1-84550-192-1

The Word Became Fresh

How to Preach from Old Testament Narrative Texts

Dale Ralph Davis

...I still believe that traditional Old Testament criticism has had the effect of killing the Old Testament for the church. This little tome can hardly reverse that, but it is meant as an exercise in reading the Old Testament for fun and profit. As my mother-in-law used to say, 'It's different anyway.' And maybe it will help. Most of what I do in the following pages involves discussing examples of Old Testament narratives. I have tried to select examples from a broad range of possibilities. By the way, I assume that you have the biblical text handy in order to carry on your 'Berean' work.

Dale Ralph Davis,
Minister in Residence, First Presbyterian Church, Columbia, South Carolina

I think Davis succeeds admirably in his goal. I found myself stirred up reading the book. He writes well and shows how, even though there are difficult and confusing parts of Scripture, it is not that difficult to find key truths. This is a very encouraging and helpful book.

Ray Van Neste,
Director, R. C. Ryan Center for Biblical Studies,
Union University, Jackson, Tennessee

There is no more gifted expositor of the Old Testament in our day than Ralph Davis. His book not only brings scholarly research to bear on the subject, but also reflects his many years of preaching week after week through the Old Testment. What a gift to the church to have such a fine book.

Richard Pratt,
President, Third Millennium Ministries, Orlando, Florida

Christian Focus Publications

Our mission statement –

STAYING FAITHFUL

In dependence upon God we seek to impact the world through literature faithful to His infallible Word, the Bible. Our aim is to ensure that the Lord Jesus Christ is presented as the only hope to obtain forgiveness of sin, live a useful life and look forward to heaven with Him.

Our books are published in four imprints:

CHRISTIAN
FOCUS

Popular works including biographies, commentaries, basic doctrine and Christian living.

CHRISTIAN
HERITAGE

Books representing some of the best material from the rich heritage of the church.

MENTOR

Books written at a level suitable for Bible College and seminary students, pastors, and other serious readers. The imprint includes commentaries, doctrinal studies, examination of current issues and church history.

CF4•K

Children's books for quality Bible teaching and for all age groups: Sunday school curriculum, puzzle and activity books; personal and family devotional titles, biographies and inspirational stories – because you are never too young to know Jesus!

Christian Focus Publications Ltd,
Geanies House, Fearn, Ross-shire,
IV20 1TW, Scotland, United Kingdom.
www.christianfocus.com